# WinterSong

# Winter Song

## Christmas Readings by
## Madeleine L'Engle &
## Luci Shaw

Harold Shaw Publishers
Wheaton, Illinois

Copyright © 1996 by Harold Shaw Publishers

ISBN 0-87788-855-8

Cover flap photo © 1996 by Maria Rooney
Cover and inside design by David LaPlaca
Compiled by Lil Copan

**Library of Congess Cataloging-in-Publication Data**

Wintersong : Christmas readings / Madeleine L'Engle and Luci Shaw.
     p.  cm.
   ISBN 0-87788-855-8
   1. Christmas—Literary collections. 2. Winter—Literary collections. 3. American literature—20th century. I. L'Engle, Madeleine. Selections. 1996. II. Shaw, Luci. Selections. 1996.
PS509.C56W56 1996
810.8'035—dc20                                   96-28370
                                                   CIP

03  02  01  00  99  98  97  96

10  9  8  7  6  5  4  3  2  1

# BY MADELEINE L'ENGLE

# BY LUCI SHAW

# Contents

# Unraveling a Season

## Early Winter

## SUMMER'S END

Now the long golden shadows of evening no longer stretch across the field. Shadows already hover in the corners. Nevertheless we set the table for dinner outdoors. It is cool enough so that I put on my old polo coat. My feet in summer sandals are cool. Long before we finish eating we have to light the hurricane lamps. We sit there watching the last pale light leave the sky, the first stars tremble into the darkness. Then the Big Dipper is there, and Cassiopeia's Chair, brilliant against the night. Summer is over.

—*ML'E*

## A FEATHERED CAROL

Between fence posts the five strands of wire are strung with

twenty black birds—nervous quarter-notes perched on a musical

staff—a measure of sparrows—a score to serenade the season—

a treble obbligato—a feathered carol marked *tutti, con anime,*

*presto agitato, crescendo*—until the sudden *finale* of wings . . .

—*LS*

## GOLDEN DELICIOUS

Last night's killing frost uncolored
the whole of the Skagit. This afternoon,
hiking the valley, I found
a spread of apple trees gone wild—
black nets of branches
heavy with yellow fruit, frozen
solid enough to last the winter.

If the freeze had held them
in its hand, vise-hard, not let go . . .

But a rogue river of wind, come loose
from the Sound at noon, began
to thaw the valley rotten.
Now the numbed apples are falling,
one, one, one, till the gray ground boils
with bruised gold, hanging the old orchard's
autumn air with the winy smell of loss.

*—LS*

## NOVEMBER 3

*for Esther-Marie Daskalakis*

Crickets
are past carding in
our summer songs.
The season
is unravelling
before our eyes, rotting
as the fabric
of the field
rots. All that is
asked of us now
is that we spin
the crumpled threads,
& weave
the filaments & fibers—
sage, burnt
umber, sapphire blue—
into a curtain for
our winter view.

—LS


## A THANKSGIVING WEEKEND

Snow fell on Friday, a lovely clinging whiteness that outlined
every twig and branch and blade of grass. Now we have had rain
and the snow is all gone, but it was just right for a Thanksgiving
weekend in the country.

—ML'E

# AN ASTONISHING BRILLIANCE

As I came home from getting mail at the office at noon, sleet filled the air and bounced off the windshield, then turned to large, soft flakes that began to fall so thickly that in minutes they were piled inches deep on the road, coating every stone and branch. The landscape became a monochrome patterned with intricate blacks and grays against the matte white. The few splashes of color that remained—the solitary diamond of the yellow road sign, the jewel of the flashing red light at North and Fair Oaks, the clusters of scarlet high-bush cranberries—achieved an astonishing brilliance.

Then, just as suddenly as it began, the snow shower stopped, the air cleared, and the gray sky turned all pearly, full of pink light so luminous, like the inside of a shell, that even the snow-piled branches showed dark against it.

—LS

# A CHILD'S PRAYER

Thank you, God, for water,
for the water of the ocean
in which I paddle with my bare feet
and let the sand squish through my toes.
Thank you for the water from the brook
which flows even in the winter
under the ice.

—ML'E

*for Madeleine*

Behind me—a thud
on the sidewalk, padded with
leaves like open hands.

I turn. It is like
a key. The jade womb unlocks
birthing you at my feet.

New as a baby
you hold the heavy secrets
of growing, dying.

Now fingered and shrunk,
your Fall gloss faded, you look
as spent as I feel,

But still you ride my
raincoat pocket—Christ's coal for
my five cold fingers.

It was late autumn in Vancouver, a hiatus of chilling rain—the year too far gone for warmth and golden days, too early for Christmas.

I left a friend's house after a very early-morning Great Books discussion group, descended the wooden steps, and moved along the walk toward my car. Under my feet the concrete sidewalk felt mushy. Looking down, I realized that it was so thickly carpeted with wide, yellow chestnut leaves that the pavement was completely covered. The parent chestnut tree loomed above me, muddy gold in the early gray of the rain-filled dawn. A long day of reading, tutorials, and teaching lay before me. I was already tired. It was cold. I shivered.

Then, I felt as much as heard a faint plop behind me. As I

turned and looked back, the green, spiny husk of the chestnut that had just thudded on the leaves split open, and the glossy, brown nucellus rolled toward me, as if heaven had not only dropped me a gift but had unwrapped it to save me the trouble.

I love chestnuts, the silk feel of them, their pregnant weight, their uneven roundness, their satin shine. This one seemed to gleam with potential life at a time of year when everything else was dying or rotting or going to sleep. I picked up the small present and put it in my raincoat pocket. My day had been renewed.

In time my chestnut lost some of its plump gloss, but it stayed in my pocket all winter. Every time I fingered it I was warmed by the thought of its Giver and the timing of the gift.

—LS

## THAT TINY FLAME

I think of James Clement (in *The Love Letters* and *Certain Women*) telling about the making of cider in the winter, when it is put outdoors to freeze. In the center of the frozen apple juice is a tiny core of pure flame that does not freeze. My faith (which I enjoy) is like that tiny flame. Even in the worst of moments it has been there, surrounded by ice, perhaps, but alive.

—ML'E

# FROSTY

my winter
breath
is making
small ghosts
out of
night air

unsure of
their shape
they drift
dissolving
in thin
moonlight

leaves of
dark poplars
nod
endlessly
in the wind
rustling yes
yes yes
you've almost
got it

but with lips
stiff as
frozen petals
I give up on
ghosts
try a whistle
to turn
breathing
into something
warm

*—LS*

# WHITE ON BLACK

The monody of cats feuding in the outside
    stairwell
splits the night between the brick walls.
The sinewy sounds rise—a vortex of wails—
through the cold window behind my headboard,
    like
a predator dream itching to expose itself,
clawing at my consciousness. I know the why
of my panic: the nightmare of being
shut in a box with this fierce shadow.

Then the white princess, softest of house cats,
cracks the door, insinuates herself almost
without sound, bumps up onto the bed.
Her eyes, lenses of the night, scan
the dim room (as is her habit) for some dusky
    garment
on which to shed her white fur, like a skin
of frost. Instead, she finds me, claims the hollow
of my body for her nest. Like a blotter
I absorb the warmth of paws, the rhythm of
push and pull, familiar as breathing.
Sleep falls kindly as snow, a drift of silk.

When I wake to the faint alarm of sunlight
across the sheets, the ticking clock has
    crystallized
the air. The cat is gone, having printed
my black sweater on the floor with her
faint shape in white. The way dreams evaporate
with waking. The way the only scrap we keep
is the memory of having dreamt.

—LS

## NIGHT THROUGH
## A FROSTY WINDOW

galaxies glisten
across glass

the constellations
crowd between
clustered frost beads
tangle in their
ice-bright fringes

inches from my face
sealed-in stars
play with the planets

two kinds of tingling light
touch fingers
kiss in my eye

focusing
near to far
to near
tells me
they are worlds apart

but
melted by a breath
see
again
now they all swim together
on the dark pane

It was one of my favorite places in our old house—the little
landing halfway up the stairs. There through the evening window I could see the whole wide sky uninterrupted by streetlights
or lights from other houses.

One severely cold winter all the windows in the house were
decorated with flakes and scrolls of frost like a baroque patterned

foil, all silver and white. That night I stood on the landing and looked out through the glass, between the stars of frost, to where, millions of light years away, the stars twinkled through space. The infinitely far stars seemed as close to my eyes as the tiny touches of frost on the glass. And when I breathed on them, lightly and warmly, they melted and melded, swimming together, the very far joined to the very near.

Years later, after photography had become my passion, I loved to record on film this aspect of the cold. The images were clearest on early mornings, with the rising sun highlighting the window frost. The marvel was that once again the far and the near, the immense and the infinitesimal, the powerful and the fragile were collaborating to create a moment of beauty and revelation for me. The sun was in service to these small frost feathers—lighting them into radiance. Is it fanciful for me to think of the sun on the frost as a metaphor of God's face shining on me, small and insignificant as I am?

—LS

## WINTER NAP

Winter afternoon.
A thick quilt.
A meditating cat
sealing the crack of air
between bed and
body. Under
the massage of paws
even the cramped heart
relents, blessed
by the prayer of purr.

—LS

# THE GLORY

Without any rhyme
without any reason
my heart lifts to light
in this bleak season

Believer and wanderer
caught by salvation
stumbler and blunderer
into Creation

In this cold blight
where marrow is frozen
it is God's time
my heart has chosen

In paradox and story
parable and laughter
find I the glory
here in hereafter

—ML'E

The sky is black as an empty heart.
The sky is pierced with stars loud as angels,
And all I can exclaim to myself is *Mirabile!*
This is a time of premonition, and sharp surprise,
and scurrying feet.

From the eaves icicles fall and break with
the tinkle of bells.
In the wind dead leaves scatter, spent as straw in
a dull manger.
All I can mutter is *Amen!*
This is a month of frosts, and rebuff,
and questions hard as birth.

Astonishment—as a baby bursts bloody from
the womb.
Air spins from his fresh lungs like a word
so that all we can chant—a mass in A minor—
is *Kyrie:*
This is a season of serial visions, and a bodily God,
and a sword in the heart.

—*LS*

# THE DOOR, THE WINDOW

To get older is to watch the door close
inch by inch against my will
so that the in-flow of silky air stops, and the
sounds of woods, of creek water.
In the small house of my ear I listen to the message
of blood, knowing others are deaf to it, as I
begin to be to their soft speech across

the dinner table. My memory thins; names drift
just beyond the rim of recollection. I'm told
the floaters in my right eye are only gel thickening
into dark splinters that diminish the light.
"Nothing can be done," my doctor says. "You'll
get used to them." I am not getting used to them.

My years undermine me, eating away in the dark
silent as carpenter ants in the beams. The pine mirror
in the bathroom reflects my white slackness; why
are my cells failing me just when I am
getting the hang of their glistening life? The minutes
wear me away—a transparent bar of glycerin soap,

a curved amber lozenge dissolving
in daily basins of water. The window glass, brittle
as the scalloped collars of ice that shrink our stream,
still opens its icon eye to me, allows me to see
across the sun-struck grass, white with frost, to hear
the water telling its winter story, telling mine.

—LS

# WINTER NIGHTS

*for Kristin*

Your father, when he died,
left this behind, his *head thing*
he called it—a square
of knitted wool, beige, blue,

to tuck around his head
like a small rug. I finger it
now, (the stitches like
his body cells, like all

the intricate minutes of his life),
almost the way I fingered it
growing on the needles,
knitting for him a meager defense

against those Illinois nights
in December when he'd wake
with a headache
from the cold. Afterwards

I slept with it hugged
to my chest like a stuffed
animal—a brief blanket for
my heart, a comfort, like him.

—*LS*

## BENEDICTION:
## THE GRACE OF SALT

The world is white with the salt of the Lord,
and look—the heavens are shaking again!
These darkening days, the flakes fall
on all our fields like a benediction. Our lips
lift to their bite, their cold salute.
We taste the fine tang in the air with tongues
eager for the sting of white to cleanse
our souls and cool our fevers, seasoning us
with snow.

—LS

# CHAPTER 2

# A Widening of the Imagination

## *Annunciation*

# THE OVERSHADOW

*". . . the power of the Most High will*
*overshadow you . . ."—Gospel of Luke*

When we think of God, and
angels, and the Angel,
we suppose ineffable light.

So there is surprise in the air
when we see him bring to Mary,
in her lit room, a gift of darkness.

What is happening under that
huge wing of shade? In that mystery
what in-breaking wildness fills her?

She is astonished and afraid; even in
that secret twilight she bends her head,
hiding her face behind the curtain

of her hair; she knows that
the rest of her life will mirror
this blaze, this sudden midnight.

—LS

# A WIDENING OF THE IMAGINATION

It came to me, recently, that faith is "a certain widening of the imagination." When Mary asked the Angel, "How shall these things be?" she was asking God to widen her imagination.

All my life I have been requesting the same thing—a baptized imagination that has a wide enough faith to see the numinous in the ordinary. Without discarding reason, or analysis, I seek from my Muse, the Holy Spirit, images that will open up reality and pull me in to its center.

This is the benison of the sacramental view of life.

—*LS*

# ANNUNCIATION

1

Sorrowfully
the angel appeared
before the young woman
feared
to ask what must be asked,
a task
almost too great to bear.
With care,
mournfully,
the angel bare
the tidings of great joy,
and then
great grief.
Behold, thou shalt conceive.
Thou shalt bring forth a son.
This must be done.
There will be no reprieve.

2

Another boy
born of woman (who shall also grieve)
full of grace
and innocence
and no offence—
a lovely one
of pure and unmarked face.

3

How much can a woman bear?

## 4

Pain will endure for a night
but joy comes in the morning.

His name is Judas.

That the prophets may be fulfilled
he must play his part.
It must be done.
Pain will endure.
Joy comes in the morning.

—*ML'E*

# TOO MUCH TO ASK

It seemed too much to ask
of one small virgin
that she should stake shame
against the will of God.
All she had to hold to
were those soft, inward
flutterings
and the remembered sting
of a brief junction—spirit
with flesh.
Who would think it
more than a dream wish?
an implausible, laughable
defense.

And it seems much
too much to ask me
to be part of the
different thing—
God's shocking, unorthodox,
unheard of Thing
to further heaven's hopes
and summon God's glory.

—LS

# OPPOSING PARALLELS:
## A JOURNAL ENTRY

A group of us from Regent and Vancouver School of Theology went to an excellent production of *Much Ado about Nothing* at Bard on the Beach. I've always loved the play because of Beatrice and Benedick, Beatrice being one of the best, funniest, and warmest of Shakespeare's women's roles.

Hero, Beatrice's cousin, and Claudio come off much less well. Hero is set up by the villain to look as though she is being unfaithful to her fiancé on the eve of their wedding. Claudio believes the cruel hoax without question and then, with vicious cruelty, allows the wedding to take place as planned until the moment when the friar asks if anyone knows of any impediment, at which point he brutally and publicly denounces the innocent Hero.

It reminded me of another man whose fiancée seems to have betrayed him at the last minute. Instead of denouncing her, having her stoned—the customary punishment for adultery—he lovingly decides to send her away to some safe place.

And then he is willing to believe the angel who tells him not to be afraid to take the young girl for his wife, for the child within her is from God.

I wonder if Shakespeare was aware of the opposing parallels?

—*ML'E*

# BEARER OF LOVE

The great swan's wings were wild as he flew down;
Leda was almost smothered in his embrace.
His crimson beak slashed fiercely at her gown—
lust deepened by the terror on her face.

Semele saw her lover as a god.
Her rash desire was blatant, undenied.
He showed himself, thunder and lightning shod.
Her human eyes were blasted and she died.

And Mary sat, unknowing, unaware.
The angel's wings were wilder than the swan
as God broke through the shining, waiting air,
gave her the lily's sword thrust and was gone.

The swans, the old gods fall in consternation
at the fierce coming of the wild wind's thrust
entering Mary in pure penetration.
The old gods die now, crumbled stone and rust.

Young Mary, moved by Gabriel, acquiesced,
asked nothing for herself in lowliness,
accepted, too, the pain, and then, most blest,
became the bearer of all holiness.

*—ML'E*

# THE LABORS OF ANGELS*

Plucking our meager treasures, grain
by grain, we disregard celestial messengers
to our jeopardy.

Sexless and muscular, angels
must wrestle, pitting light against
sinew and darkness. They arrive
without notice, blazing, terrifying us
with good news.

Barren or virgin
we bear our improbable children,
and angels raise heaven like a song.
Still, angels can weep;
in your mind's eye, see
their clear, mineral tears.

Against the indigo sky,
where judgment pulses
like an aneurysm, sunlight spins
its horizontal threads across the field until
the yellows in the standing wheat stalks
match the low light. Harvester angels
cast huge wings of shadow,
scything a crop, lifting it
from the skin of an acre
like fleece from a sheep's flank.

It is only later that they delicately
unhook teasel, thistle, burdock
from the heavy gold grain.

—LS

*Upon seeing the painting by Roger Wagner, "The Harvest Is the End of the World and the
Reapers Are Angels."

# Angels

*He makes his angels winds, . . . flames of fire, . . .*
*spirits in the divine service.—Hebrews*

ften today we see angels respresented as miniature dolls with wings, perched atop Christmas trees, molded in gilded papier-mâché or plastic, blowing trumpets, strumming harps, or cupping candles. We think of them as *pretty!*

Sometimes they show up as babies—chubby cherubs, gilded and poised on our infant's nursery wall, or in a crèche, or in some medieval church building or fresco—whimsical, decorative, harmless, charming, even *cute*.

In fact, popular culture almost equates angels with the good fairies in children's stories, complete with gauzy wings and magical powers. Today's angels seem to serve no evident, overarching, divine purpose. Like neighborhood convenience stores, they exist to provide whatever we want, when we want it. They are domesticated, friendly, providing a non-judgmental 12-step program, or a heavenly squad of cheerleaders. This is angelology without theology, angels detached from God.

Yet, what is an angel truly like? The Bible tells us that, contrary to this prevailing image of convenience and accommodation, angels are powerful, forceful servants of the Almighty—"They excel in strength." Madeleine L'Engle writes, "All the angelic host, as they are described in Scripture, have a wild and radiant power that often takes us by surprise." They *have* to be strong and powerful—as Martin Luther wrote: "How earnestly the angels strive for us against the devil! How hard a combat it is!"

In the book of Revelation, where we find that extraordinary phrase, "war in heaven," it is the archangel Michael and his angels who fight and win against the devil and his angels. Enormous power. Holiness. Beauty. Radiance. High voltage energy. Those are the truer, more appropriate descriptive words for angels.

Though angels are often depicted with beautiful women's faces, biblical angels are neither male nor female; masculinity and femininity are not categories we can apply to angels, nor are they sexual beings in the human sense; like God, they seem to be above, or beyond gender. Anthropomorphize them as we may, (that is, imagine them in terms of human personality and physiology), when it comes to their reality we can only *guess* at what they might look like or act like if we could see them as clearly as we see other human beings.

The earliest angel we find in the book of Genesis is described like this: "At the east of the garden of Eden [God] placed the cherubim, and a sword flaming and turning to guard the way to the tree of life" —a kind of divine security guard.

From then on, throughout the Bible, we keep meeting angels—three of them visiting Lot to warn him and his family to escape from Sodom and Gomorrah; a huge angel wrestling with Jacob all night long, so powerfully that Jacob came away from that encounter with a permanently damaged thighbone, but in the process both his nature and his name were changed for the good; commissioning and preparing Gideon to fight the enemies of the Hebrew people. Angels showed up to encourage the prophet Elijah, running away from wicked king Ahab and queen Jezebel. An angel appeared to Balaam's ass, blocking the pathway, in that famous story of a prophet who thought he knew better than God. During a time of transition and uncertainty for the people of

Israel, an angel directed the mission of the prophet Isaiah when King Uzziah died. Daniel tells how an angel kept him company, protecting him in the den of lions, where he'd been imprisoned by another wicked king. After Jesus' temptation by the Devil, "angels ministered to him" during the following forty days in the wilderness. And an angel was powerful enough to roll back the heavy stone to Jesus' tomb after the Resurrection. In the Acts of the Apostles there's the wonderful story of Peter's being released from prison by an angel, who opened before him a series of prison doors, saving him from execution by King Herod, and leading him to freedom.

Clearly, their strength is primarily used not to destroy us, but to help, guide, protect, and guard us, as God's beloved children. In the story of Hagar and her son Ishmael, dying of thirst in the desert, an angel showed her where there was a spring of water, saving both their lives.

The Bible is *crowded* with angels—angels in ranks of hierarchy—seraphim, cherubim, thrones, dominions, virtues, powers, principalities, angels, and archangels. Tradition names the four most prominent archangels—Gabriel, Michael, Raphael, and Uriel, as the four who support God's throne.

One warning. Angels are God's representatives, not God-substitutes. Sometimes in popular culture we tend to credit angels for deliverance or enlightenment rather than the Holy Spirit, or Christ the Savior. Such angelolatry is perverse. It is always God to whom praise and thanks should rise.

The word *angel* or *angels* appears 340 times in Scripture. But what does the word *angel* mean? It comes from the Greek word *angelos*, meaning a messenger carrying a message from God to human beings. These message-carriers are swift, sure, strong, and timely as we read in the Psalms:

> Bless the LORD, O you his angels,
>    you mighty ones who do all his bidding,
>    obedient to his spoken word.
> Bless the Lord, all his hosts,
>    his ministers that do his will.

and in the book of Hebrews:

> *Of the angels he says,*
> *"He makes his angels winds,*
> *and his servants flames of fire."*

> *Are not all angels spirits in the divine service, sent to serve*
> *for the sake of those who are to inherit salvation?*

What would it have been like for the people in the Bible who met an angel? We've seen what angels *aren't*—all the popular stereotypes. And we need to rescue angels from this distorted imagery and try to get back to what we know about the members of the angelic host.

First of all, what do angels look like? Perhaps we want them to look human, like us, because then they won't seem so—*unlike* us. But though most artists represent angels with bodies and faces and expressions that look human, the Bible's descriptions suggest how different they are from us.

Here's how Isaiah saw it:

> *Seraphs were in attendance above [the Lord]; each had six*
> *wings: with two they covered their faces, and with two they*
> *covered their feet, and with two they flew. And one called*
> *to another and said:*

> > "Holy, holy, holy is the Lord of hosts; the whole earth
> > is full of his glory."

And from the prophet Ezekiel we get another view of these "living creatures" (which means they too were created by God, though different from us). Here's what he says:

> *As I looked, a stormy wind came out of the north: a great*
> *cloud with brightness around it and fire flashing forth con-*
> *tinually, and in the middle of the fire, something like gleam-*
> *ing amber. In the middle of it was something like four living*

*creatures. This was their appearance: they were of human form. Each had four faces and each of them had four wings. Their legs were straight, and the soles of their feet were like the sole of a calf's foot; and they sparkled like burnished bronze. Under their wings on their four sides they had human hands. And the four had their faces and their wings thus: their wings touched one another; each of them moved straight ahead, without turning as they moved. As for the appearance of their faces: the four had the face of a human being, the face of a lion on the right side, the face of an ox on the left side, and the face of an eagle; such were their faces. Their wings were spread out above; each creature had two wings, each of which touched the wing of another, while two covered their bodies. Each moved straight ahead; wherever the spirit would go, they went, without turning as they went. In the middle of the living creatures there was something that looked like burning coals of fire, like torches moving to and fro among the living creatures; the fire was bright, and lightning issued from the fire. The living creatures darted to and fro, like a flash of lightning.*

*As I looked at the living creatures, I saw a wheel on the earth beside the living creatures, one for each of the four of them. As for the appearance of the wheels and their construction: their appearance was like the gleaming of beryl; and the four had the same form, their construction being something like a wheel within a wheel. When they moved, they moved in any of the four directions without veering as they moved. Their rims were tall and awesome, for the rims of all four were full of eyes all around. . . . Wherever the spirit would go, they went, and the wheels rose along with them; for the spirit of the living creatures was in the wheels. . . . and there was a splendor all around. Like the bow in a cloud on a rainy day, such was the appearance of the splendor all around.*

Ezekiel was plainly mystified but fascinated by such a vision. Though he made valiant attempts to describe his vision in all its bizarre detail, he keeps using the phrase "something like" because an exact description was impossible. A contemporary artist, Gary Panter, interprets Ezekiel's words, painting his conjectures at an even further remove—this is pretty wild and weird stuff! Definitely un-human!

But all these words piled on words, images piled on images, are efforts to suggest or define or describe something indescribable, something outside of our experience. Writers down the ages have hazarded guesses about angels. And all the human representations of angels, in painting, sculpture, stained glass, literature, have been just that—guesses.

Such guesses have certainly caught the public up in a frenzy of interest: the play *Angels in America* capitalized on the obsession; a recent Boston Museum of Fine Arts catalog had four pages of angel jewelry, ties, scarves, tree ornaments, and address books; the bookstores are full of angel books; The Museum Store at Stanford had a whole window display of angel books, each of them different. I have reviewed two new books about angels, both by friends of mine; both *Time* and *Newsweek* recently have had cover stories on angels and the supernatural. There's even a magazine called *Angels in Review* which attempts to keep up with current angelic news stories. Angels have become celebrities.

But there have been *serious* attempts to understand angels. C. S. Lewis, in one of his time-and-space trilogy novels, *Out of the Silent Planet,* tells how his hero, Ransom, encounters creatures on Mars called *eldila*. His representation gives us an interesting alternate impression of heavenly beings who are beyond human comprehension, or even description. Ransom "seemed to hear, against the background of morning silence, a faint, continual agitation of silver sound—hardly a sound at all . . . and yet impossible to ignore." And he made out only "slight variations of light and shade which no change in the sky accounted for. . . . Like the silvery noises in the air, these footsteps of light were shy of observation."

And in his subsequent novel *Perelandra,* Lewis adds to this perception of *eldila*:

*The sound was astonishingly unlike a voice. It was. . . , I suppose, rather beautiful. But it was . . . inorganic. . . . This was . . . as if rock or crystal or light had spoken of itself. And it went through me from chest to groin like the jolt that goes through you when you think you have lost your hold while climbing a cliff.*

*That is what I heard. What I saw was simply a very faint rod or pillar of light. . . . it had two other characteristics which were less easy to grasp. One was its colour. Since I saw the thing I must obviously have seen it either white or coloured; but no efforts of my memory can conjure up the faintest image of what that colour was. . . . The other was its angle. It was not at right angles to the floor. . . . What one actually felt . . . was that the column of light was vertical but that the floor was not horizontal . . . [as if] this creature had reference to some horizontal, to some whole system of directions based outside the Earth. . . . I had not doubt at all that I was seeing an eldil.*

Bible stories about angels portray them as pretty startling. Think of all the stories of angels who appeared to people in the early chapters of Saint Luke's Gospel, which tells the Christmas story:

- Zechariah, in the Temple, was "startled and gripped with fear" when Gabriel made his sudden appearance and announced that Zechariah and his wife, Elizabeth, were to have a baby. And the angel said, FEAR NOT!

- Mary, a young girl, was "greatly troubled" at being told by an angel that before she was to marry her fiancé, Joseph, she would have a baby whose father was God. And the angel said, FEAR NOT!

- The shepherds on the midnight hillside outside Bethlehem "were terrified" when an angel appeared in the night sky to tell them of the baby Jesus' birth and then, even more terrifying, "a multitude of the heavenly host" joined the first angel and started to praise God with sound that filled the hills with angel sound. But the angel said, FEAR NOT!

In every case in St. Luke's account, the angel needed to calm some degree of human anxiety and consternation with the words "Fear not," or "Don't be afraid" before voicing a momentous message direct from God.

> *when an angel*
> *snapped the old thin threads of speech*
> *with an untimely birth*
> *announcement, slit*
> *the seemly cloth of an even*
> *more blessed event with*
> *shears of miracle,*
> *invaded the privacy of a dream,*
> *multiplied*
> *to ravage the dark silk of the sky, the*
> *innocent ears*
> *with swords of sound:*
> *news in a new dimension demanded*
> *qualification.*
> *The righteous were as vulnerable as others.*
> *They trembled for those strong*
> *antecedent* fear nots, *whether goat-*
> *herds, virgins, workers in wood or*
> *holy barren priests.*
>
> *in our nights our*
> *complicated modern dreams rarely*
> *flower into visions. No*
> *contemporary Gabriel*
> *dumbfounds our worship, or burning,*
> *visits our bedrooms. No*
> *sign-post satellite hauls us, earth-bound but*

*star-struck, half*
*around the world with hope.*
*Are our sensibilities*
*too blunt to be assaulted*
*with spatial power-plays and far-out*
*proclamations of peace? Sterile,*
*skeptics, yet we may be broken*
*to his slow silent birth*
*(new-torn, new-*
*born ourselves at his*
*beginning new in us.)*
*His bigness may still burst*
*our self-containment*
*to tell us—without angels' mouths—*
fear not.

*God knows we need to hear it, now*
*when he may shatter*
*with his most shocking coming*
*this proud cracked place*
*and more if, for longer waiting,*
*he does not.*

Daniel, telling of his vision of an angel, "standing before me, looking something like a man" became "frightened and fell prostrate." He says, "I fell face to the ground. Then he touched me and set me on my feet and said, 'Listen, and I will tell you what will take place later. . . .'"

And St. John, the aging apostle exiled on the island of Patmos, saw a vision full of brilliant light and heat and rushing sound, and a being with a face "like the sun shining with full force," who told him, twice, "Don't be afraid; write what you see."

As C. S. Lewis says about the great lion Aslan, in the *Chronicles of Narnia,* angels are not safe (in the sense that they're not comfortable and manageable), but they're good. And knowing that they are *good* is much more important, in the long run, than feeling that they are *safe.* It's all right for us to feel a healthy respect, even an awe, of angels. But their power is on God's side, so we needn't fear them if we, too, are on God's side.

It's interesting to me that though angels move faster, see further, are seemingly immortal (we never hear of angels dying), and have far greater power than we humans do, *they don't know everything*. For instance, according to the first letter of St. Peter, they don't understand the mystery of Incarnation and redemption.

*Seeing Creation come, they know it well:*
*the stars, the shoots of green shine for them*
*one by one. They have eternity to learn*
*the universe, which once encompassing, angels*
*forget not. Clean as steel wires, shining*
*as frost, making holiness beautiful, aiming*
*at the Will of God like arrows flaming*
*to a target, earthly solidity presents no*
*barrier to their going. Easily they slope*
*through the rind of the world, the atoms*
*pinging in their celestial orifices. Matter*
*& anti-matter open before them like a Bible.*
*Inhabiting the purposes of God, Who is*
*the Lord of all their Hosts, in Deep Space*
*their congregation wages war with swords of fire*
*& power & great joy, seizing from the*
*Hierarchies of Darkness Andromeda's boundaries*
*& all constellations. The rising Day Star*
*is their standard bearer, as on earth they stay*
*the Adversary's slaughter of the Sons of God.*

*Praise*
*is their delight also. Rank on rank they sing*
*circularly around the Throne, dancing together*
*in a glory, clapping hands at all rebellion*
*repented of, or sheep returned. They who*
*accompany the bright spiriting up of a redeemed*
*swimmer from the final wave, who trace*
*the grey, heavy clot that marks the drowning*
*of the profane to his own place—how can we*
*think to escape their fiery ministry? We listen*

for their feathers, miss the shaft of light
at our shoulder. We tread our gauntlet paths
unknowing, covered by shields of angels. (The ass
sees one & shames us for blindness.) "Fear not's
unfurl like banners over their appearing, yet
we tremble at their faces.
　　　　　　　　Seraphim sing
in no time zone. Cherubim see as clearly on
as back, invest acacia planks with arkhood in
their certainty (whose winged ornamenting gilds
the tabernacle shade). Comprehending the
compacted plan centered in every seed, the grown
plant is no more real to them & no surprise.
Dampened by neither doubt nor supposition,
they understand what happens to a worm. And if
we ask—Did he please God? Did he fulfill
the Eternal Plan for worms, drilling the soil,
digesting it? & his strange hermaphroditic
replication—did he do it well? & what will
happen to his wormy spirit when he shrivels back
to soil? heavenly Beings answer instantly,
giving God high praise for faithful worms.
The archangel sees with eyes quicker than ours &
unconfused by multiplicity. For him, reality's
random choice is all clear cause & effect:
each star of snow tells of intelligence; each
cell carries its own code; at a glance he knows
from whence the crests of all the wrinkles on
the sea rebound. He has eternity to tell
it all, & to rejoice.
　　　　　　　　But what is this
conjunction of straw & splendor? The echo of
sharp laughter from a crowd (of men bent from
the image of the firstmade man) as nails
pierce flesh, pierces the Bright Ones with
perplexity. They see the Maker's hands helpless
against Made Wood. The bond is sealed with

*God's blood. Thus is Love's substance darkness to their light. The Third Day sweetens the deep Riddle. Heralds now of a new Rising, they have eternity to solve it, & to praise.*

Can we see angels today? Frederick Buechner says:

*People see only what they expect to see. . . . Since we don't expect to see [angels], we don't. An angel spreads his glittering wings over us, and we say things like, "It was one of those days that made you feel good just to be alive," or "I had a hunch everything was going to turn out all right," or "I don't know where I ever found the courage, but I did."*

Angels are never there just to beautify our greeting cards or our church decor. They are often our protectors, and nearly always their appearance brings significant news from God that demands human response or action. The book of Hebrews tells us they have been sent "to serve for the sake of those who are to inherit salvation."

Are angels our guardians? The one biblical clue I have found is in the Gospel of Matthew where Jesus says: "Take care that you do not despise one of these little ones; for, I tell you, in heaven their angels continually see the face of my Father in heaven . . . it is not the will of your Father in heaven that one of these little ones should be lost."

At this time of Advent, we watch for angels not only as we celebrate the playing out of the historical drama of the Incarnation, but in our own lives. Be alert for God's surprises—messengers with messages that will startle us out of our complacency. My prayer for you, for me, for all those we love, is:

*"Lord, make us aware of the realities we cannot see. Send your messengers to us today, to help us, to protect us and give us courage, to remind us of your love."*

—LS

# O SIMPLICITAS

An angel came to me
and I was unprepared
to be what God was using.
Mother I was to be.
A moment I despaired,
thought briefly of refusing.
The angel knew I heard.
According to God's Word
I bowed to this strange choosing.

A palace should have been
the birthplace of a king
(I had no way of knowing).
We went to Bethlehem;
it was so strange a thing.
The wind was cold, and blowing,
my cloak was old, and thin.
They turned us from the inn;
the town was overflowing.

God's Word, a child so small
who still must learn to speak
lay in humiliation.
Joseph stood, strong and tall.
The beasts were warm and meek
and moved with hesitation.
The Child born in a stall?
I understood it: all.
Kings came in adoration.

Perhaps it was absurd;
a stable set apart,
the sleepy cattle lowing;
and the incarnate Word
resting against my heart.
My joy was overflowing.
The shepherds came, adored

the folly of the Lord,
wiser than all men's knowing.

—*ML'E*

## THE OTHER SIDE OF REASON

To paint a picture or to write a story or to compose a song is an incarnational activity. The artist is a servant who is willing to be a birthgiver. In a very real sense the artist (male or female) should be like Mary, who, when the angel told her that she was to bear the Messiah, was obedient to the command.

Obedience is an unpopular word nowadays, but the artist must be obedient to the work, whether it be a symphony, a painting, or a story for a small child. I believe that each work of art, whether it is a work of great genius, or something very small, comes to the artist and says, "Here I am. Enflesh me. Give birth to me." And the artist either says, "My soul doth magnify the Lord," and willingly becomes the bearer of the work, or refuses; but the obedient response is not necessarily a conscious one, and not everyone has the humble, courageous obedience of Mary.

As for Mary, she was little more than a child when the angel came to her; she had not lost her child's creative acceptance of the realities moving on the other side of the everyday world. We lose our ability to see angels as we grow older, and that is a tragic loss.

God, through the angel Gabriel, called on Mary to do what, in the world's eyes, is impossible, and instead of saying, "I can't," she replied immediately, "Be it unto me according to thy Word."

How difficult we find the Annunciation. How could one young, untried girl contain within her womb the power which created the galaxies? How could that power be found in the helplessness of an infant? It is more than we, in our limited, literal-mindedness, can cope with, and so we hear, "I can't be a Christian because I can't believe in the virgin birth," as though faith were something which lay within the realm of verification. If it can be verified, we don't need faith.

I don't need faith to know that if a poem has fourteen lines, a specific rhyme scheme, and is in iambic pentameter, it is a sonnet; it may not be a good sonnet, but it will be a sonnet. I don't need faith to know that if I take flour and butter and milk and seasonings and heat them in a double boiler, the mix will thicken and become white sauce. Faith is for that which lies on the *other* side of reason. Faith is what makes life bearable, with all its tragedies and ambiguities and sudden, startling joys. Surely it wasn't reasonable of the Lord of the Universe to come down and walk this earth with us and love us enough to die for us and then show us everlasting life? We will all grow old, and sooner or later we will die, like the old trees in the orchard. But we have been promised that this is not the end. We have been promised life.

What would have happened to Mary (and to all the rest of us) if she had said *No* to the angel? She was free to do so. But she said, *Yes*. She was obedient, and the artist, too, must be obedient to the command of the work, knowing that this involves long hours of research, of throwing out a month's work, of going back to the beginning, or, sometimes, scrapping the whole thing. The artist, like Mary, is free to say *No*. When a shoddy novel is published the writer is rejecting the obedient response, taking the easy way out. But when the words mean even more than the writer knew they meant, then the writer has been listening. And sometimes when we listen, we are led into places we do not expect, into adventures we do not always understand.

Mary did not always understand. But one does not have to understand to be obedient. Instead of understanding—that intellectual understanding which we are so fond of—there is a feeling of rightness, of knowing, knowing things which we are not yet able to understand.

A young woman said to me, during the question-and-answer period after a lecture, "I read *A Wrinkle in Time* when I was eight or nine. I didn't understand it, but I knew what it was about."

As long as we know what it's about, then we can have the courage to go wherever we are asked to go, even if we fear that the road may take us through danger and pain.

—*ML'E*

## More than We Can Do

We are all asked to do more than we can do. Every hero and heroine of the Bible does more than he would have thought it possible to do, from Gideon to Esther to Mary.

—*ML'E*

## Virgin

As if until that moment
nothing real
had happened since Creation

As if outside the world were empty
so that she and he were all
there was—he mover, she moved upon

As if her submission were the most
dynamic of all works; as if
no one had ever said Yes like that

As if one day the sun had no place
in all the universe to pour its gold
but her small room

—*LS*

# CHAPTER 3

# Breaking Space and Time

*Advent*

O Oriens

*Transformation*

*Advent visitation*

*Redeeming All Brokenness*

*Salutation*

*Time and Space Turned Upside Down*

*Advent, 1971*

*Forever's start*

*Solstice*

# *O ORIENS*

O come, O come Emmanuel
within this fragile vessel here to dwell.
O Child conceived by heaven's power
give me thy strength: it is the hour.

O come, thou Wisdom from on high;
like any babe at life you cry;
for me, like any mother, birth
was hard, O light of earth.

O come, O come, thou Lord of might,
whose birth came hastily at night,
born in a stable, in blood and pain
is this the king who comes to reign?

O come, thou Rod of Jesse's stem,
the stars will be thy diadem.
How can the infinite finite be?
Why choose, child, to be born of me?

O come, thou key of David, come,
open the door to my heart-home.
I cannot love thee as a king—
so fragile and so small a thing.

O come, thou Day-spring from on high:
I saw the signs that marked the sky.
I heard the beat of angels' wings
I saw the shepherds and the kings.

O come, Desire of nations, be
simply a human child to me.
Let me not weep that you are born.
The night is gone. Now gleams the morn.

Rejoice, rejoice, Emmanuel,
God's Son, God's Self, with us to dwell.

—*ML'E*

## TRANSFORMATION

We are now in Advent. The readings in the *Lectionary* start back at the beginning again. The Christmas tree has been bought. From where I write I can see it through the sliding door of the family room, sitting on the porch with the first snow sifting through it. The house, which is being transformed with Christmas decorations, is in chaos, like a woman caught in the middle of doing her hair.

*—LS*

# ADVENT VISITATION

Even from the cabin window I sensed the wind's
contagion begin to infect the rags of leaves.
Then the alders gilded to it, obeisant, the way

angels are said to bow, covering their faces with
their wings, not solemn, as we suppose, but
possessed of a sudden, surreptitious hilarity.

When the little satin wind arrived
I felt its slide through the cracked-open door,
(a wisp of prescience? a change in the weather?)

and after the small push of breath—You
entering with your air of radiant surprise;
I the astonished one.

These still December mornings
I fancy I live in a clear envelope of angels
like a cellophane womb. Or a soap bubble,

the colors drifting, curling. Outside
everything's tinted rose, grape, turquoise,
silver—the stones by the path, the skin of sun

on the pond ice, at the night the aureola of
a pregnant moon, like me, iridescent,
almost full term with light.

—LS

As we move into Advent we are called to listen, something we seldom take time to do in this frenetic world of over-activity. But waiting for birth, waiting for death—these are listening times, when the normal distractions of life have lost their power to take us away from God's call to center in Christ.

During Advent we are traditionally called to contemplate death, judgment, hell, and heaven. To give birth to a baby is also a kind of death—death to the incredible intimacy of carrying a child, death to old ways of life and birth into new—and it is as strange for the parents as for the baby. Judgment: John of the Cross says that in the evening of life we shall be judged on love; not on our accomplishments, not on our successes and failures in the worldly sense, but solely on love.

Once again, as happened during the past nearly two thousand years, predictions are being made of the time of this Second Coming, which, Jesus emphasized, "even the angels in heaven do not know." But we human creatures, who are "a little lower than the angels," too frequently try to set ourselves above them with our predictions and our arrogant assumption of knowledge which God hid even from the angels. Advent is not a time to declare, but to listen, to listen to whatever God may want to tell us through the singing of the stars, the quickening of a baby, the gallantry of a dying man.

Listen. Quietly. Humbly. Without arrogance.

In the first verse of *Jesu, Joy of Man's Desiring,* we sing, "Word of God, our flesh that fashioned with the fire of life impassioned," and the marvelous mystery of incarnation shines. "Because in the mystery of the Word made flesh," goes one of my favorite propers, for it is indeed the mystery by which we live, give birth, watch death.

When the Second Person of the Trinity entered the virgin's womb and prepared to be born as a human baby (a particular baby, Jesus of Nazareth), his death was inevitable.

It is only after we have been enabled to say, "Be it unto me according to your Word," that we can accept the paradoxes of Christianity. Christ comes to live with us, bringing an incredible promise of God's love, but never are we promised that there will be no pain, no suffering, no death, but rather that these very griefs are the road to love and eternal life.

In Advent we prepare for the coming of all Love, that love which will redeem all the brokenness, wrongness, hardnesses of heart which have afflicted us.

—*ML'E*

## SALUTATION

Framed in light,
Mary sings through the doorway.
Elizabeth's six month joy
jumps, a palpable greeting,
a hidden first encounter
between son and Son.

And my heart turns over
when I meet Jesus
in you.

—*LS*

A *dvent.* That time of waiting, waiting even more trembling and terrible than the waiting between Good Friday and Easter Sunday.

But what are we waiting for? Why? We're not waiting, as we so often are taught as children, for Christmas, for the baby Jesus to be born in a stable in Bethlehem. We're waiting for something that has not happened yet, that has never happened before, something totally new. We know only what the end of this waiting has been called throughout the centuries: The Second Coming.

What is it, the coming of Christ in glory? The return of Christ to the earth? What's it going to be like? We don't know. We don't know anything about this event that is new, that has never before happened.

But, being human and therefore curious, we want to know. We want to know so badly that sometimes we think we do know, and that can sometimes lead to danger and even evil. Whenever we want to know something before its true time, we get into trouble. We've never learned how to wait. We're impatient creatures. Our impatience, our unwillingness to wait, is all through our stories, from Adam and Eve on.

The only thing I know about the Second Coming is that it is going to happen because of God's love. God made the universe out of love; the Word shouted all things joyfully into being because of love. The Second Coming, whenever it happens and whatever it means, will also be because of love.

We express what we believe in icons, which are creative, or idols, which are destructive. But what is a constructive icon?

Icons break time and space. One of my favorite icons is Reblev's famous picture of the Trinity, the three heavenly angels who came to visit Abraham and Sarah sitting at a table in front of the tent. On the table is the meal that has been prepared for the heavenly visitors, and what is this meal? We look at the table and see chalice and paten, the bread and the wine. Time and space turned upside down. Here, three thousand years before the birth of Christ, is the Trinity, Father, Son, and Holy Spirit; here, three thousand years before Jesus came into time for us, is the body and the blood.

So what could be an icon of the Second Coming? I think of Creation itself, and how little the astrophysicists know about it. It does seem that there was, indeed, a moment of Creation, when something, so subatomically tiny as to be almost nothing at all, suddenly opened up to become everything. How long did it take? There wasn't any time before the beginning. Time began with the beginning. Time will end at the ending, at the Second Coming.

On a rare, clear night I look at the stars. According to present knowledge, all the stars are rushing away from each other at speeds impossible for us to conceive. Are they going to keep on, getting further and further away, more and more separate? Or is there going to be a point at which the procedure is reversed, and they start coming together again? Nobody knows.

The metaphor that has come to me is birth. Our ordinary (oh, no, they're not ordinary at all—they're extraordinary) human births. Right now I am like the unborn baby in the womb, knowing nothing except the comforting warmth of the amniotic fluid in which I swim, the comforting nourishment entering my body from a source I cannot see or understand. My whole being comes from an unseen, unknown nurturer. By that nurturer I am totally loved and protected, and that love is forever. It does not end when I am precipitated out of the safe waters of the womb into the unsafe world. It will not end when I breathe my last, mortal breath. That love manifested itself joyously in the creation of the universe, became particular for us in Jesus, and will show itself most gloriously in the Second Coming. We need not fear.

There are many tough questions for which we have no finite, cut and dried answers. Even Jesus did not answer all our questions! But he came, because of that love which casts out fear. He came, and he will come again.

Even so, come Lord Jesus!

—ML'E

# ADVENT, 1971

When will he come
and how will he come
and will there be warnings
and will there be thunders
and rumbles of armies
coming before him
and banners and trumpets
When will he come
and how will he come
and will we be ready

O woe to you people
you sleep through the thunder
you heed not the warnings
the fires and the drownings
the earthquakes and stormings
and ignorant armies
and dark closing on you
the song birds are falling
the sea birds are dying
no fish now are leaping
the children are choking
in air not for breathing
the aged are gasping
with no one to tend them

a bright star has blazed forth
and no one has seen it
and no one has wakened

—*ML*

# FOREVER'S START

The days are growing noticeably shorter; the nights are longer, deeper, colder. Today the sun did not rise as high in the sky as it did yesterday. Tomorrow it will be still lower. At the winter solstice the sun will go below the horizon, below the dark. The sun does die. And then, to our amazement, the Son will rise again.

> Come, Lord Jesus, quickly come
> In your fearful innocence.
> We fumble in the far-spent night
> Far from lovers, friends, and home:
> Come in your naked, newborn might.
> Come, Lord Jesus, quickly come;
> My heart withers in your absence.
>
> Come, Lord Jesus, small, enfleshed
> Like any human, helpless child.
> Come once, come once again, come soon:
> The stars in heaven fall, unmeshed:
> The sun is dark, blood's on the moon.
> Come, Word who came to us enfleshed,
> Come speak in joy untamed and wild.
>
> Come, thou wholly other, come,
> Spoken before words began,
> Come and judge your uttered world
> Where you made our flesh your home.
> Come, with bolts of lightning hurled,
> Come, thou wholly other, come,
> Who came to man by being man.
>
> Come, Lord Jesus, at the end,
> Time's end, my end, forever's start.
> Come in your flaming, burning power.
> Time, like the temple veil, now rend;
> Come, shatter every human hour.

Come, Lord Jesus, at the end.
Break, then mend the waiting heart.

—*ML'E*


# SOLSTICE

Winter solstice, when the sun seems to stand still in heaven, watching for the Baby to be born.

—*LS*

CHAPTER 4

# Marvelous Mystery

*Incarnation*

# THIS EXTRAORDINARY BIRTH

The Nativity is a time to take courage. How brave am I? Can I bear, without breaking apart, this extraordinary birth?

*—ML'E*

## INTO THE DARKEST HOUR

It was a time like this,
War & tumult of war,
a horror in the air.
Hungry yawned the abyss—
and yet there came the star
and the child most wonderfully there.

It was time like this
of fear & lust for power,
license & greed and blight—
and yet the Prince of bliss
came into the darkest hour
in quiet & silent light.

And in a time like this
how celebrate his birth
when all things fall apart?
Ah! wonderful it is
with no room on the earth
the stable is our heart.

*—ML'E*

# SHINE IN THE DARK I

From a dark dust of stars
kindled one, a prick of light.
Burn! small candle star,
burn in the black night.

In the still hushed heart
(dark as a black night)
shine! Savior newly born,
shine till the heart's light!

*—LS*


# SHINE IN THE DARK II

Into the blackness breached with white
the star shivers like a bell.
God of birth and brightness
bless the cool carillon
singing into sight!
Plot its poised pointing flight!

Dark has its victories
tonight, in David's town.
But the star bell's tongue
trembles silver still
in your felicity.

*—LS*

## Shine in the dark III

The stars look out on
roofs of snow.
They see the night,
a velvet glow
with amber lanterns
shining so.

God searches through
the sweep of night.
Is there a heart burns
warm and bright
to warm God's own heart
at the sight?

*—LS*

## After annunciation

This is the irrational season
When love blooms bright and wild.
Had Mary been filled with reason
There'd have been no room for the child.

*—ML'E*

# STORY

When we try to define and over-define and narrow down, we lose the story the Maker of the Universe is telling us in the Gospels. I do not want to explain the Gospels; I want to enjoy them.

And that is how I want to read and write story. This does not mean that story deals only with cheeriness, but that beneath the reality of life is the rock of faith. I ask God to set me upon a rock that is higher than I so that I may be able to see more clearly, see the tragedy and the joy and sometimes the dull slogging along of life with an assurance that not only is there rock under my feet, but that God made the rock and you and me, and is concerned with Creation, every galaxy, every atom and subatomic particle. Matter *matters*.

This is the promise of the Incarnation. Christ put on human matter, and what happens to us is of eternal, cosmic importance. That is what true story affirms.

—*ML'E*

# MAKER OF THE GALAXIES

O Maker of the galaxies,
Creator of each star,
You rule the mountains & the seas,
And yet—oh, here you are!

You ride the fiery cherubim
And sail on comet fall.
You teach the seraphim to hymn,
And yet—you left it all.

You left the realms of fire & ice.
Into a young girl's womb you came.
O God! *This* was the sacrifice!
Nothing will ever be the same.

—*ML'E*

Last night at a Christmas festival, I heard a choir sing, in Latin, Gabrielli's *O Magnum Mysterium*: "O greatest of mysteries and O most wonderful sacrament, Jesus lying there in the manger for all creatures to gaze upon. O blessed virgin, whose womb was deemed worthy of bearing Christ, the Lord Jesus. Alleluia!" An intense sweetness filled the space in that auditorium as voices deep, strong, high, clear, resonant, and reverent moved out from the stage and enfolded me. The harmony and the all-encompassing sense of the meaning of the words, which went beyond intellectual understanding, pierced me.

The Incarnation shows us simply, clearly, what would otherwise blind us—Jesus, Logos, metaphor of God, Word that both tells and shows, accessible yet mysterious, essence as well as sacrament, actuality and analogy both.

God and his truth are like a sun that fills the sky. His huge verities flare off from its center of certainty like the flaming tongues of a corona, overwhelming us in our insignificance. Yet he may appear to those whose eyes are open—the seers (Annie Dillard calls herself a stalker of truth, Virginia Stem Owens a spy)—in forms as unthreatening, yet true, as a baby, or a seed, or a dove, or a lamb, or a loaf of bread. Or a flick of rainbow color on the wall.

—LS

## FIRST COMING

He did not wait till the world was ready,
till men and nations were at peace.
He came when the Heavens were unsteady,
and prisoners cried out for release.

He did not wait for the perfect time.
He came when the need was deep and great.
He dined with sinners in all their grime,
turned water into wine. He did not wait

till hearts were pure. In joy he came
to a tarnished world of sin and doubt.
To a world like ours, of anguished shame
he came, and his Light would not go out.

He came to a world which did not mesh,
to heal its tangles, shield its scorn.
In the mystery of the Word made Flesh
the Maker of the stars was born.

We cannot wait till the world is sane
to raise our songs with joyful voice,
for to share our grief, to touch our pain,
He came with Love: Rejoice! Rejoice!

—ML'E

## A GALAXY, A BABY

The birth of my own babies (every woman's Christmas) shows me
that the power which staggers with its splendor is a power of love,
particular love. Surely it takes no more creative concentration to
make a galaxy than a baby. And surely the greatest strength of all
is this loving willingness to be weak, to share, to give utterly.

—ML'E

The second Christmas of our marriage, and the first with our six-month-old baby, the beautiful flesh of our child made the whole miracle of incarnation new for me, and that newness touched on *kairos*, (God's time, not human time).

Now, all these years later, I plunge into the delightful business of painting Christmas ornaments with my grandchildren; I hear the hammer as Bion puts together a dolls' house which looks remarkably like Crosswicks, our house in the country; the New York kitchen smells fragrant with Christmas cookies; this, for me, is incarnation.

—*ML'E*

# IMPOSSIBLE THINGS

In Lewis Carroll's *Alice's Adventures Through the Looking Glass,* the White Queen advises Alice to practice believing six impossible things every morning before breakfast. It's good advice. Unless we practice believing in the impossible daily and diligently, we cannot be Christians, those strange creatures who proclaim to believe that the Power that created the entire universe willingly and lovingly abdicated that power and became a human baby.

Particle physics teaches us that energy and matter are interchangeable. So, for love of us recalcitrant human creatures, the sheer energy of Christ changed into the matter of Jesus, ordinary human matter, faulted, flawed, born with the seed of death already within the flesh as a sign of solidarity with our mortality.

But this birth also promises us that our human, mortal matter is permeated with Christ's total energy, the creative energy which shouted into being all the galaxies, hydrogen clouds, solar systems, planets, all life—even us! When Christ was born as Jesus, born of a human mother as all babies are born, that incredible birth honored all our births, and assured us that we, God's beloved children, partake of eternal life. For indeed it follows that as Christ partook of human life, we partake of the divine life.

How can we trivialize the Incarnation as we have done? Tawdry tinsel and crowded shopping malls are not the worst of it. Arguing about Christ's divinity versus Jesus' humanity is equally to miss the point. Like the White Queen we need merrily to accept the impossible (with us it is impossible; with God nothing is impossible!): the baby who was born two thousand years ago in Bethlehem was God, come to us as a human babe. Jesus: wholly human. It's more than our puny minds can comprehend. It's one reason Jesus kept insisting that we be as little children, because we can understand this wonder only with childheartedness, not with grown-up sophistication.

We can, to some extent, understand Jesus' humanity. We can glory in but not understand, in any cognitive way, his divinity.

We are still like that fetus in the womb, comfortably swimming around in the warm amniotic fluid, with no idea of what life out of the womb is going to be like. Unlike us grown-ups, the fetus seems to enjoy *being* without questions! Questions are fine as long as we do not insist on finite answers to questions which are infinite. How could Jesus be wholly God and wholly human? What does the resurrection of the body mean? How can God be good if terrible things are allowed to happen? How much free will do we have? Can we make a difference?

To that last question, at least, we can say Yes, and that Yes is easier for us to say because of Christmas. What a difference this birth makes to our lives! God, in human flesh, dignifies our mortal flesh forever. How did the schism between flesh and spirit ever come about to confuse and confound us? God put on our flesh and affirmed its holiness and beauty. How could we ever have fallen for the lie that spirit is good and flesh is evil? We cannot make our flesh evil without corrupting spirit, too. Both are God's and both are good, as all that our Maker made is good.

God created, and looked on Creation, and cried out, It is good!

At Christmastime we look at that tiny baby who was born in Bethlehem, and we, too, may cry out, It is good! It is very good!

—*ML'E*


## A LIVING METAPHOR

In the Incarnation, Christ became a living metaphor—the Word. Jesus took the risk of reducing himself to what we could see and touch and listen to, a living message that bridged the huge communication gap between deity and humankind.

—*LS*

# THE BETHLEHEM
# EXPLOSION

*And it came to pass in those days that there went out a decree from Caesar Augustus, that all the world should be taxed. And Joseph also went up from Galilee . . . to be taxed, with Mary his espoused wife, being great with child.—Gospel of Luke*

The chemistry lab at school
was in an old greenhouse
surrounded by ancient live oaks
garnished with Spanish moss.

The experiment I remember best
was pouring a quart of clear fluid
into a glass jar, and dropping into it,
grain by grain, salt-sized crystals,
until they layered
like white sand on the floor of the jar.

One more grain—and suddenly—
water and crystal burst
into a living, moving pattern,
a silent, quietly violent explosion.
The teacher told us that only when
we supersaturated the solution,
would come the precipitation.

The little town
was like the glass jar in our lab.
One by one they came, grain by grain,
all those of the house of David,
like grains of sand to be counted.

The inn was full. When Joseph knocked,
his wife was already in labour; there was no room
even for compassion. Until the barn was offered.

That was the precipitating factor. A child was born,
and the pattern changed forever, the cosmos
shaken with that silent explosion.

*—ML'E*


# THE PROMISE OF HIS BIRTH

In the beginning I was confused and dazzled,
a plain girl, unused to talking with angels.
Then there was the hard journey to Bethlehem,
and the desperate search for a place to stay,
my distended belly ripe and ready for deliverance.
In the dark of the cave, night air sweet with the moist breath
of the domestic beasts, I laughed, despite my pains,
at their concern. Joseph feared that they would frighten me
with their anxious stampings and snortings,
but their fear was only for me, and not because of me.
One old cow, udders permanently drooping,
lowed so with my every contraction
that my own birthing cries could not be heard,
and so my baby came with pain and tears and much hilarity.

Afterwards, swaddled and clean, he was so small and tender
that I could not think beyond my present loving
to all this strange night pointed. The shepherds came,
clumsy and gruff, and knelt and bought their gifts,
and, later on, the Kings; and all I knew was marvel.
His childhood was sheer joy to me. He was merry and loving,
moved swiftly from laughters to long, unchildlike silences.
The years before his death were bitter to taste.
I did not understand, and sometimes thought that it was he
who had lost sight of the promise of his birth.

*—ML'E*

## IN HUMAN FLESH

The enfleshing of the Word which spoke the galaxies made the death of that Word inevitable. All flesh is mortal, and the flesh assumed by the Word was no exception in mortal terms. So the birth of the Creator in human flesh and human time was an event as shattering and terrible as the *eschaton*. If I accept this birth I must accept God's love, and this is pain as well as joy because God's love, as I am coming to understand it, is not like human love.

—*ML'E*

## CROSSING THE SPACE

There is always a gap between present reality and future potential.

A gift unwrapped has never been truly received. An uncashed check cannot be spent. A bridge that spans a raging river is useless to us unless we begin to advance across it.

The divide between earth and heaven, between us and God, is one that only Jesus Christ could reconnect. He is our link to life and eternity—a bridge to be stepped onto so that it bears our whole weight as we cross the space from one side to the other.

—*LS*

## MADE FLESH

After
the bright beam of hot annunciation
fused heaven with dark earth
his searing, sharply focused light
went out for a while
eclipsed in amniotic gloom:
his cool immensity of splendor
his universal grace
small-folded in a warm dim
female space—
the Word stern-sentenced
to be nine months dumb—
infinity walled in a womb
until the next enormity—
the Mighty, after submission
to a woman's pains
helpless on a barn-bare floor
first-tasting bitter earth.

Now
I in him surrender
to the crush and cry of birth.
Because eternity
was closeted in time
he is my open door
to forever.
From his imprisonment my freedoms grow,
find wings.
Part of his body, I transcend this flesh.
From his sweet silence my mouth sings.
Out of his dark I glow.
My life, as his,

slips through death's mesh,
time's bars,
joins hands with heaven,
speaks with stars.

—*LS*

## O SAPIENTIA

It was from Joseph first I learned
of love. Like me he was dismayed.
How easily he could have turned
me from his house; but, unafraid,
he put me not away from him
(O God-sent angel, pray for him).
Thus through his love was Love obeyed.
The Child's first cry came like a bell:
God's Word aloud, God's Word in deed.
The angel spoke: so it befell,
and Joseph with me in my need.
O Child whose father came from heaven,
to you another gift was given,
your earthly father chosen well.

With Joseph I was always warmed
and cherished. Even in the stable
I knew that I would not be harmed.
And, though above the angels swarmed,
man's love it was that made me able
to bear God's love, wild, formidable,
to bear God's will, through me performed.

—*ML'E*

We often think of Jesus' suffering on this earth. Sometimes we forget that most of what we know about Mary, Jesus' mother, is also in the context of pain. Even her name means "bitter."

Her role was a difficult one from the start. Young and inexperienced, she was called by the Lord's angel to a pregnancy that owned no human father and opened her to charges of promiscuity. Her vocation was to be the mother of a paradox—God in a man's body, a man who would be considered a failed rebel by the leaders in his day, and finally a criminal.

Early on, she must have felt dismay at having to travel to Bethlehem in her ninth month, of giving birth in the most primitive and comfortless of conditions, of knowing later that her own little one survived at the life cost of Bethlehem's baby boys who were slaughtered by Herod in Jesus' place.

On the eighth day after Jesus' birth a prophecy laced with further torment was spoken to Mary: "A sword will pierce your own soul"—a pain for her to ponder and dread for over thirty years. During that waiting time, Jesus directed some of his hardest sayings to his gentle mother—words that must have wounded. But the culmination of all her anguish was at the cross, under its very arm, as she watched her beloved son die a slow and brutal death.

But hers was not the kind of dead-end pain that has no meaning. She was privileged to be caught up in the life of the One who fought the fierce battle between light and darkness. We can understand that mix of pain and joy only as we carry Christ in our hearts, birthing him into a hostile world. That may mean suffering; we may be as misunderstood as Mary. But there is a reward: *Because eternity was closeted in time, he is our open door to forever.*

—*LS*

# MARY SPEAKS

O you who bear the pain of the whole earth,
  I bore you.
O you whose tears give human tears their worth,
  I laughed with you.
You, who, when your hem is touched, give power,
  I nourished you.
Who turn the day to night in this dark hour,
  light comes from you.
O you who hold the world in your embrace,
  I carried you.
Whose arms encircled the world with your grace,
  I once held you.
O you who laughed and ate and walked the shore,
  I played with you.
And I, who with all others, you died for,
  now I hold you.

May I be faithful to this final test:
in this last time I hold my child, my son,
his body close enfolded to my breast,
the holder held: the bearer borne.
Mourning to joy: darkness to morn.
Open, my arms: your work is done.

—ML'E

# MARY'S SONG

Blue homespun and the bend of my breast
keep warm this small hot naked star
fallen to my arms. (Rest . . .
you who have had so far
to come.) Now nearness satisfies
the body of God sweetly. Quiet he lies
whose vigor hurled
a universe. He sleeps
whose eyelids have not closed before.

His breath (so slight it seems
no breath at all) once ruffled the dark deeps
to sprout a world.
Charmed by doves' voices, the whisper of straw,
he dreams,
hearing no music from his other spheres.
Breath, mouth, ears, eyes
he is curtailed
who overflowed all skies,
all years.
Older than eternity, now he
is new. Now native to earth as I am, nailed
to my poor planet, caught that I might be free,
blind in my womb to know my darkness ended,
brought to this birth
for me to be new-born,
and for him to see me mended
I must see him torn.

*—LS*

# THIS TINY BABY

Whoever is the baby?
Nothing but a little lamb
who says God is and that I am.

Who is this tiny baby?
Just an infant, meek and mild,
just a feeble, mortal child.

Who is this tiny baby?
The Lord strong and mighty
even the Lord mighty in battle.

The king of glory's coming
who is this
even the Lord of Hosts
This is the tiny baby!

—*ML'E*

# AN OPEN WINDOW

If I look for an icon for Christmas, what I see is a mother and child and the radiant love between them—not necessarily Mary, the mother of God, but any one of us human mothers holding our babe in delight and joy.

This icon, too, alas, can be idol. When a mother manipulates, controls, abuses, ignores, dominates, sees her own motherhood as more important than the child she has birthed, idolatry is again rampant. But the icon can remain clear even when we make mistakes, as all mothers do, as even Mary surely did. She, being human, could not comprehend the dual nature of her son. She wanted him to turn water into wine, to reveal his divinity, even though he made it quite clear that the time was not ready. We mortal mothers far too often do not want our children to be human. We are human creatures, and with the best will in the world we do the wrong things. But as long as we remember that Creation, including our children, is God's, not ours, the icon of mother and child can be an open window.

—*ML'E*

# THE FIRST-BORN LIGHT

The Maker's hand flung stars across the night
with angels bursting forth from galaxies
new music singing from the spheres in harmonies
that blessed the dancing of the first-born light.

And then the light was darkened by an earth
dimmed by torn dreams, saddened by shrill pride.
Stars faded, lost their story, and died.
The dance distorted in strange lies and anger.
Love's hand again was lifted. In a manger
Again the Maker of the stars gave birth.

—*ML'E*

# CREED

In the creed, as I say it each day, I affirm that "I believe in the resurrection of the body." We don't know how that body is going to be resurrected, or what it is going to be like. But if the Apostle Paul could believe in a *spiritual body* so, most of the time, can I. It is yet another mystery of the Word made flesh.

By whatever name it is called—a creed, affirmation, or statement of faith—most religious establishments express what they believe in one way or another. And these expressions are all inadequate. What we hold in common is the affirmation of our faith in the mystery of the Word made flesh.

When Paul was asked for explanations, his wonderful (and sensible) reply was, "Don't be silly."

—*ML'E*

## IT IS AS IF INFANCY WERE THE WHOLE OF INCARNATION

This time of the year
the new-born child
is everywhere,
planted in madonnas' arms
hay mows, stables,
in palaces or farms,
or quaintly, under snowed gables,
gothic angular or baroque plump,
naked or elaborately swathed,
encircled by Della Robbia wreaths,
garnished with whimsical
partridges and pears,
drummers and drums,
lit by oversize stars,
partnered with lambs,
peace doves, sugar plums,
bells, plastic camels in sets of three
as if these were what we needed
for eternity.

But Jesus the Man is not to be seen.
There are some who are wary, these days,
of beards and sandalled feet.

Yet if we celebrate, let it be
that He
has invaded our lives with purpose,
striding over our picturesque traditions,
our shallow sentiment,
overturning our cash registers,
wielding His peace like a sword,
rescuing us into reality,
demanding much more
than the milk and the softness
and the mother warmth

of the baby in the storefront crèche,
(only the Man would ask
all, of each of us)
reaching out
always, urgently, with strong
effective love
(only the Man would give
His life and live
again for love of us).

Oh come, let us adore Him—
Christ—*the Lord.*

—*LS*

Observe and contemplate.
Make real. Bring to be.
Because we note the falling tree
The sound is truly heard.
Look! The sunrise! Wait—
It needs us to look, to see,
To hear, and speak the Word.

Observe and contemplate
The cosmos and our little earth.
Observing, we affirm the worth
Of sun and stars and light unfurled.
So, let us, seeing, celebrate
The glory of Love's incarnate birth
And sing its joy to all the world.

Observe and contemplate.
Make real. Affirm. Say Yes,
And in this season sing and bless
Wind, ice, snow; rabbit and bird;
Comet, and quark; things small and great.
Oh, observe and joyfully confess
The birth of Love's most lovely Word.

*—ML'E*

Thank you, God, for being born,
You who first invented birth
(Universe, galaxies, the earth).
When your world was tired & worn
You came laughing on the morn.

Thank you, most amazing Word
For your silence in the womb
Where there was so little room
Yet the still small voice was heard
Throughout a planet dark & blurred.

Merry Christmas! Wondrous day!
Maker of the universe,
You the end, & you the source
Come to share in human clay
And, yourself, to show the Way.

—*ML'E*

# CHAPTER 5

# Circled with Light

*Christmas Celebrations*

# The Glorious Mystery

Rise up, with willing feet
Go forth, the Bridegroom meet:
  Alleluia!
Bear through the night
Your well-trimmed light,
Speed forth to join the marriage rite.

All hail, Incarnate Lord,
Our crown, and our reward!
  Alleluia!
We haste along,
In pomp of song,
And gladsome join the marriage throng.

Lamb of God, the heav'ns adore thee,
And men and angels sing before thee,
  With harp and cymbal's clearest tone.
By the pearly gates in wonder
We stand, and swell the voice of thunder
  That echoes round thy dazzling throne.
No vision ever brought,
No ear hath ever caught
    Such rejoicing:
We raise the song, We swell the throng,
To praise thee ages all along. Amen.*

---

*Wachet Auf (Sleepers, Wake) by Philip Nicolai; translated by Catherine Winkworth.

*You shall know him when he comes*
*Not by any din of drums*
*Nor by the vantage of His airs*
*Nor by anything he wears—*
*Neither by his crown—*
*Nor his gown—*
*For his Presence known shall be*
*By the Holy Harmony*
*That His coming makes in thee.* *

Who was he, this tiny babe whose birth we celebrate at Christmas time, whose Resurrection lightens our hearts at Easter, and whose coming in glory we await?

He was born, as we are all born, of water and blood, of a human mother, a young girl whose courage is awesome. It was a difficult birth in those days when often women and infants did not survive childbirth. Mary was not able to have her baby at home. Her mother was not able to be with her, to comfort her. There was no trained midwife or doctor. She lived in a small country, an outpost in the Roman Empire, and when Rome declared a census, there was no excuse: Mary and Joseph were required to go to Bethlehem and register, because Joseph was *of the house of David.*

The closest we can come to understanding what it is like to be controlled by an alien power is to think of Poland or France under Nazi domination; of countries such as Albania, taken over by the Soviet Union. The ordinary people, living and working and loving and birthing, don't get consulted on these matters.

Mary and Joseph were just such ordinary people. Joseph was a carpenter, and solidly middle class. And when Rome said, "Come and be counted," they had no choice.

And so, as the Gospel of Luke tells us, it was while they were in Bethlehem, that the time came for Mary to deliver. *And she brought forth her firstborn son, and wrapped him in swaddling clothes, and laid him in a manger, because there was no room for them in the inn.*

---

*Unknown 15th century writer

The manger was likely in a cave in the hills, rather than in the kind of barn we see today. When I was in Jerusalem I saw similar caves for domestic animals, built into the hillside, and outlined with the golden stones of that blue and gold land.

*Of the Father's love begotten,*
*Ere the worlds began to be,*
*He is Alpha and Omega,*
*He the source, the ending he,*
*Of the things that are, that have been,*
*And that future years shall see,*
*Evermore and evermore!*

*O that birth forever blessed,*
*When the Virgin, full of grace,*
*By the Holy Ghost conceiving,*
*Bore the Saviour of our race;*
*And the Babe, the world's Redeemer,*
*First revealed his sacred face,*
*Evermore and evermore!*

*O ye heights of heav'n adore him;*
*Angel hosts, his praises sing;*
*Powers, dominions, bow before him,*
*And extol our God and King;*
*Let no tongue on earth be silent,*
*Every voice in concert ring,*
*Evermore and evermore!*

*Thee let old men, thee let young men,*
*Thee let boys in chorus sing;*
*Matrons, virgins, little maidens,*
*With glad voices answering:*
*Let their guileless songs re-echo,*
*And the heart its music bring,*
*Evermore and evermore!*

*Christ, to thee with God the Father,*
*And, O Holy Ghost, to thee,*

*Hymn and chant and high thanksgiving,*
*And unwearied praises be:*
*Honor, glory, and dominion,*
*And eternal victory,*
*Evermore and evermore!**

This ancient hymn, written in the early centuries of Christendom, makes it very clear that Christ always was. He didn't suddenly appear in a manger in Bethlehem two thousand years ago. He was. He is. He will be. This total *is*ness is more than our finite minds can readily understand. It is nothing that can be comprehended in the language of literal thinking. But in his Gospel, Matthew quotes Jesus as saying, *I thank you, O Father, Lord of heaven and earth, because you have hidden these things from the wise and prudent, and have revealed them to children.*

If we turn away from the child, the poet, the artist in ourselves, we lose the ability to believe the glorious mysteries that lift us from being nothing more than a few nearly valueless molecules to children of light, creatures called to create along with our Creator.

So we rejoice in the mystery of this tiny baby. We give presents to each other as reminders of his great gift of himself to us. We trim the Christmas tree, although the Christmas tree was not originally a Christian symbol, but came out of northern Europe and the worship of different gods. But any affirmation of love and beauty can become Christian, because Christianity is totally committed to incarnation. The decorated tree may have secular origins, but if we truly believe in incarnation, then everything secular can also be sacred. So we trim our trees and make them sparkle with light as a symbol that light is stronger than darkness, and even in a world as dark as ours, the light still shines, and cannot be extinguished.

*This is no time for a child to be born,*
*With the Earth betrayed by war and hate*

---

*By Marcus Aurelius Clemens Prudentius; translated by John Mason Neale, Henry Williams Baker.

*And a comet slashing the sky to warn*
*That time runs out and the sun burns late.*

*That was no time for a child to be born*
*In a land in the crushing grip of Rome;*
*Honor and truth were trampled by scorn—*
*Yet here did the Saviour make his home.*

*When is the time for love to be born?*
*The inn is full on planet earth,*
*And by a comet the sky is torn—*
*Yet Love still takes the risk of birth.*

—ML'E

Particle physics has a sense of the absolute significance of the very small, the so incredibly small we can't even imagine such smallness.

In *Particles,* Michael Chester writes, "Not only does [the neutrino] have zero charge, it has zero mass. The neutrino is a spinning little bit of nothingness that travels at the speed of light."

I love that! A spinning little bit of nothingness! It so delights me that I wrote a Christmas song about it.

> The neutrino and the unicorn
> Danced the night that Christ was born.
> A spinning little bit of nothingness
> that travels at the speed of light
> an unseen spark of somethingness
> is all that can hold back the night.
> The tiny neutron split in two,
> an electron and a proton form.
> Where is the energy that is lost?
> Who can hold back the impending storm?
> Cosmic collapse would be the cost.
> A spinning nothing, pure and new,
> The neutrino comes to heal and bless.
> The neutrino and the unicorn
> danced the night that Christ was born.
> The sun is dim, the stars are few,
> The earthquake comes to split and shake.
> All purity of heart is lost,
> In the black density of night
> stars fall. O will the heavens break?
> Then through the tingling of black frost
> the unicorn in silver dress
> crosses the desert, horn alight.
> Earth's plates relax their grinding stress.
> The unicorn comes dancing to

make pure again, redeem and bless,
  The neutrino and the unicorn
  danced the night that Christ was born.

*—ML'E*


# THE BIRTH OF WONDER

When I am able to pray with the mind in the heart, I am joyfully able to affirm the irrationality of Christmas.

As I grow older
I get surer
Man's heart is colder,
His life no purer.
As I grow steadily
More austere
I come less readily
To Christmas each year.
I can't keep taking
Without a thought
Forced merrymaking
And presents bought
In crowds and jostling.
Alas, there's naught
In empty wassailing
Where oblivion's sought.
Oh, I'd be waiting
With quiet fasting
Anticipating
A joy more lasting.
And so I rhyme
With no apology
During this time
Of eschatology:

Judgment and warning
Come like thunder.
But now is the hour
When I remember
An infant's power
On a cold December.
Midnight is dawning
And the birth of wonder.

*—ML'E*

# A Full House:
# An Austin Family Story

To anybody who lives in a city or even a sizable town, it may not sound like much to be the director of a volunteer choir in a postcard church in a postcard village, but I was the choir director and largely responsible for the Christmas Eve service, so it was very much of a much for me. I settled my four children and my father, who was with us for Christmas, in a front pew and went up to the stuffy choir-robing room. I was missing my best baritone, my husband, Wally, because he had been called to the hospital. He's a country doctor, and I'm used to his pocket beeper going off during the church service. I missed him, of course, but I knew he'd been called to deliver a baby, and a Christmas baby is always a joy.

The service went beautifully. Nobody flatted, and Eugenia Underhill, my lead soprano, managed for once not to breathe in the middle of a word. The only near disaster came when she reached for the high C in *O Holy Night,* hit it brilliantly—and then down fell her upper plate. Eugenia took it in good stride, pushed her teeth back in place and finished her solo. When she sat down, she doubled over with mirth.

The church looked lovely, lighted entirely by candlelight, with pine boughs and holly banking the windows. The Christmas Eve service is almost entirely music, hence my concern; there is never a sermon, but our minister reads excerpts from the Christmas sermons of John Donne and Martin Luther.

When the dismissal and blessing were over, I heaved a sigh of relief. Now I could attend to our own Christmas at home. I collected my family, and we went out into the night. A soft, feathery snow was beginning to fall. People called out "Good-night" and "Merry Christmas." I was happily tired, and ready for some peace and quiet for the rest of the evening—our service is over by nine.

I hitched Rob, my sleeping youngest, from one hip to the other. The two girls, Vicky and Suzy, walked on either side of their grandfather; John, my eldest, was with me. They had all promised to go to bed without protest as soon as we had finished all our traditional Christmas rituals. We seem to add new ones each year, so the Christmas-Eve bedtime gets later and later.

I piled the kids into the station wagon, thrusting Rob into John's arms. Father and I got in the front, and I drove off into the snow, which was falling more heavily. I hoped that it would not be a blizzard and that Wally would get home before the roads got too bad.

Our house is on the crest of a hill, a mile out of the village. As I looked uphill, I could see the lights of our outdoor Christmas tree twinkling warmly through the snow. I turned up our back road, feeling suddenly very tired. When I drove up to the garage and saw that Wally's car was not there, I tried not to let Father or the children see my disappointment. I began ejecting the kids from the back. It was my father who first noticed what looked like a bundle of clothes by the storm door.

"Victoria," he called to me. "What's this?"

The bundle of clothes moved. A tear-stained face emerged, and I recognized Evie, who had moved from the village with her parents two years ago, when she was sixteen. She had been our favorite and most loyal baby-sitter, and we all missed her. I hadn't seen her—or heard anything about her—in all this time.

"Evie!" I cried. "What is it? What's the matter?"

She moved stiffly, as though she had been huddled there in the cold for a long time. Then she held her arms out to me in a childlike gesture. "Mrs. Austin—" She sighed as I bent down to kiss her. And then, "Mom threw me out. So I came here." She dropped the words simply, as though she had no doubt that she would find a welcome in our home. She had on a shapeless, inadequate coat, and a bare toe stuck through a hole in one of her sneakers.

I put my arms around her and helped her up. "Come in. You must be frozen."

The children were delighted to see Evie and crowded around, hugging her, so it was a few minutes before we got into the kitchen and past the dogs who were loudly welcoming us home. There were Mr. Rochester, our Great Dane; Colette, a silver-gray French Poodle who bossed the big dog unmercifully; and, visiting us for the Christmas holidays while his owners were on vacation, a ten-month-old Manchester terrier named Guardian. Daffodil, our fluffy amber cat, jumped on top of the fridge to get out of the way, and Prune Whip, our black-and-white cat, skittered across the floor and into the living room.

The kids turned on lights all over downstairs, and John called, "Can I turn on the Christmas tree lights?"

"Sure," I answered, "but light the fire first!"

I turned again to Evie, who simply stood in the middle of the big kitchen-dining room, not moving. "Evie, welcome. I'm sorry it's such chaos—let me take your coat." At first she resisted and then let me slip the worn material off her shoulders. Under the coat she wore a sweater and a plaid skirt; the skirt did not button, but was fastened with a pin, and for an obvious reason: Evie was not about to produce another Christmas baby, but she was very definitely pregnant.

Her eyes followed mine. Rather defiantly, she said, "That's why I'm here."

I thought of Evie's indifferent parents, and I thought about Christmas Eve. I put my arm around her for a gentle hug. "Tell me about it."

"Do I have to?"

103

"I think it might help, Evie."

Suzy, eight years old and still young enough to pull at my skirt and be whiny when she is tired, now did just that to get my full attention. "Let's put out the cookies and cocoa for Santa Claus *now.*"

Suddenly there was an anguished shout from the living room. "Come quick!" John yelled, and I went running.

Guardian was sitting under the tree, a long piece of green ribbon hanging from his mouth. Around him was a pile of Christmas wrappings, all nicely chewed. While we were in church, our visiting dog had unwrapped almost every single package under the tree.

Vicky said, "But we won't know who anything came from . . ."

Suzy burst into tears. "That dog has ruined it all!"

Evie followed us in. She was carrying Rob, who was sleeping with his head down on her shoulder. Father looked at her with his special warm glance that took in and assessed any situation. "Sit down, Evie," he ordered.

I took Rob from her, and when she had more or less collapsed in Wally's special chair, in front of the big fireplace, he asked, "When did you eat last?"

"I don't know. Yesterday, I think."

I dumped my sleeping child on the sofa and then headed for the kitchen, calling, "Vicky, Suzy, come help me make sandwiches. I'll warm up some soup. John, make up the couch in Daddy's office for Evie, please."

Our house is a typical square New England farmhouse. Upstairs are four bedrooms. Downstairs we have a big, rambling kitchen-dining room, all unexpected angles and nooks; a large, L-shape living room and my husband's office, which he uses two nights a week for his patients in the nearby village. As I took a big jar of vegetable soup from the refrigerator and poured a good helping into a saucepan, I could hear my father's and Evie's voices, low, quiet, and I wondered if Evie was pouring out her story to him. I remembered hearing that her father seldom came home without stopping first at the tavern and that her mother had the reputation of being no better than she should be. And yet I knew that their response to Evie's pregnancy would be one of righteous moral indignation. To my daughters I said, "There's some egg salad in the fridge. Make a big sandwich for Evie."

I lifted the curtains and looked out the window. The roads would soon be impassable. I wanted my husband to be with us, in the warmth and comfort of our home.

I went back to the stove and poured a bowl of soup for Evie. Vicky and Suzy had produced a messy but edible sandwich and then gone off. I called Evie, and she sat at the table and began to eat hungrily. I sat beside her. "How did it happen? Do I know him?"

She shook her head. "No. His name's Billy. After we left here, I didn't feel—I didn't feel that anybody in the world loved me. I think that Mom and Pop are always happiest when I'm out of the house. When I was baby-sitting for you, I thought I saw what love was like. Mrs. Austin, I was lonely, I was so lonely it hurt. Then I met Billy, and I thought he loved me. So when he wanted to—I—but then I found out that it didn't have anything to do with love, at least not for Billy. When I got pregnant, he said, well, how did I even know it was his? Mrs. Austin, I never . . . never with anyone else. When he said that, I knew it was his way of telling me to get out, just like Mom and Pop."

The girls had wandered back into the kitchen while we were talking, and Suzy jogged at my elbow. "Why does Evie's tummy look so big?"

The phone rang. I called, "John, get it, please."

In a moment he came into the kitchen, looking slightly baffled. "It was someone from the hospital saying Dad's on his way home, and would we please make up the bed in the waiting room."

Evie looked up from her soup. "Mrs. Austin—" She turned her frightened face toward me, fearful, no doubt, that we were going to put her out.

"It's all right, Evie." I was thinking quickly. "John, would you mind sleeping in the guest room with Grandfather?"

"If Grandfather doesn't mind."

My father called from the living room, "Grandfather would enjoy John's company."

"All right then, Evie." I poured more soup into her bowl. "You can sleep in John's bed. Rob will love sharing his room with you."

"But who is Daddy bringing home?" John asked.

"What's wrong with Evie's tummy?" Suzy persisted.

"And why didn't Daddy tell us?" Vicky asked.

"Tell us what?" Suzy demanded.

"Who he's bringing home with him!" John said.

Evie continued to spoon soup into her mouth, at the same time struggling not to cry. I put one hand on her shoulder, and she reached up for it, asking softly, as the girls and John went into the living room, "Mrs. Austin, I knew you wouldn't turn me out on Christmas Eve, but what about . . . well, may I stay with you for a little while? I have some thinking to do."

"Of course you can, and you do have a lot of thinking to do—the future of your baby, for instance."

"I know. Now that it's getting so close, I'm beginning to get really scared. At first I thought I wanted the baby; I thought it would make Billy and me closer, make us a family like you and Dr. Austin and your kids, but now I know that was just wishful thinking. Sometimes I wish I could just go back, be your baby-sitter again. . . . Mrs. Austin, I just don't know what I'm going to do with a baby of my own."

I pressed her hand. "Evie, I know how you feel, but things have a way of working out. Try to stop worrying, at least to-night—it's Christmas Eve."

"And I'm home," Evie said. "I feel more at home in this house than anywhere else."

I thought of my own children and hoped that they would never have excuse to say that about someone else's house. To Evie I said, "Relax then, and enjoy Christmas. The decisions don't have to be made tonight."

My father ambled into the kitchen, followed by the three dogs. "I think the dogs are telling me they need to go out," he said. "I'll just walk around the house with them and see what the night is doing." He opened the kitchen door and let the dogs precede him.

I opened the curtains, not only to watch the progress of my father and the dogs, but to give myself a chance to think about Evie and how we could help her. More was needed, I knew, than just a few days' shelter. She had no money, no home, and a baby was on the way. . . . No wonder she looked scared—and trapped. I watched the falling snow and longed to hear the sound of my husband's car. Like Vicky, I wondered who on earth he was bringing home with him. Then I saw headlights coming up the road and heard a car slowing down, but the sound was not the slightly bronchial purr of Wally's car. Before I had a chance to wonder who it could be, the phone rang. "I'll get it!" Suzy yelled, and ran, beating Vicky. "Mother, it's Mrs. Underhill."

I went to the phone. Eugenia's voice came happily over the line. "Wasn't the Christmas Eve service beautiful! And did you see my teeth?" She laughed.

"You sang superbly, anyhow."

"Listen, why I called—you have two ovens, don't you?"

"Yes."

"Something's happened to mine. The burners work, but the oven is dead, and there's no way I can get anyone to fix it now. So what I wondered is, can I cook my turkey in one of your ovens?"

"Sure," I said, though I'd expected to use the second oven for the creamed-onion casserole and sweet potatoes—but how could I say no to Eugenia?

"Can I come over with my turkey now?" she asked. "I like to put it in a slow oven Christmas Eve, the way you taught me. Then I won't have to bother you again till tomorrow."

"Sure, Eugenia, come on over, but drive carefully."

"I will. Thanks," she said.

John murmured, "Just a typical Christmas Eve at the Austins," as the kitchen door opened, and my father and the dogs came bursting in, followed by a uniformed state trooper.

When Evie saw him, she looked scared.

My father introduced the trooper, who turned to me. "Mrs. Austin, I've been talking with your father here, and I think we've more or less sorted things out." Then he looked at Evie. "Young lady, we've been looking for you. We want to talk to you about your friends."

The color drained from her face.

"Don't be afraid," the trooper reassured her. "We just want to know where we can find you. I understand that you'll be staying with the Austins for a while—for the next few weeks, at least." He looked at my father, who nodded, and I wondered what the two had said to each other. Was Evie in more trouble than I thought?

She murmured something inaudible, keeping her eyes fastened to her soup.

"Well now, it's Christmas Eve," the trooper said, "and I'd like to be getting on home. It's bedtime for us all."

"We're waiting for Daddy," Suzy said. "He's on his way home."

"And he's bringing someone with him," Vicky added.

"Looks like you've got a full house," the trooper said. "Well, 'night, folks."

My father showed him out, then shut the door behind him.

"What was that—" John started to ask.

I quickly said, "What I want all of you to do is to go upstairs, right now, and get ready for bed. That's an order."

"But what about Daddy—"

"And whoever he's bringing—"

"And reading 'The Night Before Christmas' and Saint Luke—"

"And you haven't sung to us—"

I spoke through the clamor. "Upstairs. Now. You can come back down as soon as you're all ready for bed."

Evie rose. "Shall I get Rob?" I had the feeling she wanted to get away, escape my questions.

"We might as well leave him. Vicky, get Evie some night-clothes from my closet, please."

When they had all finally trooped upstairs, including Evie, I turned to my father who was perched on a stool by the kitchen counter. "All right, Dad, tell me about it," I said. "What did the officer tell you?"

"That soup smells mighty good," he said. I filled a bowl for him and waited.

Finally he said, "Evie was going with a bunch of kids who weren't much good. A couple of them were on drugs—not Evie, fortunately, or her boyfriend. And they stole some cars, just for kicks, and then abandoned them. The police are pretty sure that Evie wasn't involved, but they want to talk to her and her friends, and they've been trying to round them up. They went to her parents' house looking for her. Her mother and father made it seem as if she'd run away—they didn't mention that they'd put her out. All they did was denounce her, but they did suggest she might have come here."

"Poor Evie. There's so much good in her, and sometimes I wonder how, with her background. What did you tell the trooper?"

"I told him Evie was going to stay with you and Wally for the time being, that you would take responsibility for her. They still want to talk to her, but I convinced him to wait until after Christmas. I guess the trooper figured that, as long as she's with you, she would be looked after and out of harm's way."

"Thank goodness. All she needs is to be hauled into a station house on Christmas Eve—" Just then the heavy knocker on the kitchen door banged.

It was Eugenia, with a large turkey in a roasting pan in her arms. "I'll just pop it in the oven," she said. "If you think about basting it when you baste yours, okay, but it'll do all right by itself. Hey you don't have yours in yet!"

What with one thing and another, I'd forgotten our turkey, but it was prepared and ready in the cold pantry. I whipped out and brought it in and put it in the other oven.

As Eugenia drove off, the dogs started with their welcoming bark, and I heard the sound of Wally's engine.

The children heard, too, and came rushing downstairs. "Wait!" I ordered. "Don't mob Daddy. And remember he has someone with him."

Evie came slowly downstairs, wrapped in an old blue plaid robe of mine. John opened the kitchen door, and the dogs went galloping out.

"Whoa! Down!" I could hear my husband command. And then,

to the children, "Make way!" The children scattered, and Wally came in, his arm around a young woman whom I had never seen before. She was holding a baby in her arms.

"This is Maria Heraldo," Wally said. "Maria, my wife, Victoria. And—" He looked at the infant.

"Pepita," she said, "After her father."

Wally took the babe. "Take off your coat," he said to the mother. "Maria's husband was killed in an accident at work two weeks ago. Her family is all in South America, and she was due to be released from the hospital today. Christmas Eve didn't seem to me to be a very good time for her to be alone."

I looked at the baby, who had an amazing head of dark hair. "She isn't the baby—"

"That I delivered tonight? No, though that little boy was slow in coming—that's why we're so late." He smiled down at the young woman. "Pepita was born a week ago." He looked up and saw our children hovering in the doorway, Evie and my father behind them. When he saw Evie, he raised his eyebrows in a questioning gesture.

"Evie's going to be staying with us for a while," I told him. Explanations would come later. "Maria, would you like some soup?"

"I would," my husband said, "and Maria will have some too." He glanced at the children. "Vicky and Suzy, will you go up to the attic, please, and bring down the cradle?"

They were off like a flash.

My husband questioned the young mother. "Tired?"

"No. I slept while the little boy was being delivered. So did Pepita." And she looked with radiant pride at her daughter who was sleeping again.

"Then let's all go into the living room and warm ourselves in front of the fire. We have some Christmas traditions you might like to share with us."

The young woman gazed up at him, at me, "I'm so grateful to you—"

"Nonsense. Come along."

Then Maria saw Evie, and I watched her eyes flick to Evie's

belly, then upward, and the two young women exchanged a long look. Evie's glance shifted to the sleeping child, and then she held out her arms. Maria gently handed her the baby, and Evie took the child and cradled it in her arms. For the first time that evening, a look of peace seemed to settle over her features.

It is not easy for a woman to raise a child alone, and Maria would probably go back to her family. In any case, her child had obviously been conceived in love, and even death could not take that away. Evie's eyes were full of tears as she carried Pepita into the living room, but she no longer looked so lost and afraid, and I had the feeling that whatever happened, Evie would be able to handle it. She would have our help—Wally's and mine—for as long as she needed it, but something told me that she wouldn't need it for long.

In a short while, Maria was ensconced in one of the big chairs, a bowl of soup on the table beside her. Evie put the baby in the cradle, and knelt, rocking it gently. Wally sat on the small sofa with Rob in his lap, a mug of soup in one hand. The two girls were curled up on the big davenport, one on either side of their grandfather, who had his arms around them. I sat across from Maria, and Evie came and sat on the footstool by me. John was on the floor in front of the fire. The only light was from the Christmas tree and the flickering flames of the fire. On the mantel were a cup of cocoa and a plate of cookies.

"Now," my husband said, "'Twas the night before Christmas, when all through the house . . . '"

When he had finished, with much applause from the children and Evie and Maria, he looked to me. "Your turn."

John jumped up and handed me my guitar. I played and sang *I Wonder as I Wander,* and then *In the Bleak Midwinter,* and ended up with *Let All Mortal Flesh Keep Silence.* As I put the guitar away, I saw Maria reach out for Evie, and the two of them briefly clasped hands.

"And now," Wally said, "your turn, please, Grandfather."

My father opened his Bible and began to read. When he came to "And she brought forth her firstborn son, and wrapped him in swaddling clothes, and laid him in a manger; because there was no room for them in the inn," I looked at Maria, who was rocking the cradle with her foot while her baby murmured in her sleep. Evie, barely turning, keeping her eyes fastened on the sleeping infant, leaned her head against my knee, rubbing her cheek against the wool of my skirt.

Suzy was sleeping with her head down in her grandfather's lap, while he continued to read: "And suddenly there was with the angel a multitude of the heavenly host praising God, and saying, Glory to God in the highest, and on earth peace, good will toward men."

I remembered John saying, "Just a typical Christmas Eve at the Austins," and I wondered if there ever could be such a thing as a typical Christmas. For me, each one is unique. This year our house was blessed by Evie and her unborn child, by Eugenia's feeling free to come and put her turkey in our stove, and by Maria and Pepita's turning our plain New England farmhouse into a stable.

—*ML'E*

## NIGHT'S LODGING

Across the purple-patterned snow
laced with light of lantern-glow,
dappled with dark,
comes Christ, the Child born from the skies.
Those are stars that are his eyes.
His baby face is wise
seen by my candle spark.
But is he cold from the wind's cold blow?
Where will he go?

I'll wrap him warm with love,
well as I'm able,
in my heart stable!

—*LS*

112

# CHRISTMAS GIFTS

And what, Lord, do you have for me?
Only a baby, helpless and small.
Shall I sit beneath this tree
And rock him till he grows up tall?

Only a baby, only a boy,
Not a mighty king or queen.
I will rock him in my joy
Underneath the tree's full green.

And what, Lord, do I have for you?
Only my arms to hold the child
Safe from winds now hurling through
The branches in this winter wild.

Only my heart, only my arms
Open to receive All Love.
How can I keep the child from harm?
How shall I all ills remove?

Child who is Love, beneath the tree
I'll sit and rock the whole night through.
Oh, what, Lord, do you have for me?
Only yourself, Lord. Only *you*.

—*ML'E*

# EIGHTY-SECOND STREET

When I remember the years in the apartment on Eighty-second Street, it is mostly the good things that I remember at home, and the bad at school. When I look at the apartment in my mind's eye, it is likely to be Christmas. This was the time when Father lifted from the physical pain in which he constantly lived, and the equally acute pain of knowing that his postwar work was not as successful as his earlier work. I did not understand my father's pain, but I knew that at Christmastime the apartment, instead of being heavy and dark, became sparkling and light as champagne, with Father sneaking home with an armload of presents, and writing stocking poems, and believing (I think) for a few weeks in a future in which there was hope.

—*ML'E*

# HOMEMADE DECORATIONS

Christmas was white this year—we had two feet of snow—with bitter cold winds, and the branches of the stripped trees like dark lace against a white sky—the first really Christmassy weather we've had for a long time. Crosswicks was filled with music, and the wonderful smell of the Christmas tree, full of ornaments that span decades, some going back to my childhood. There is one small strand of tiny, homemade silver balls, from my twelfth Christmas which was in Chamonix, Mont Blanc, where all our decorations were homemade.

—*ML'E*

# CHAMONIX

That month in Chamonix was an ambiguous one for me. When I could, I reacted as a child, but I was being forced into growing up. I wanted to balance the pain of school with comfort, safety, changelessness, but I found pain, discovery, change. I listened to Mother playing Bach on a barely playable upright piano, and I watched her play solitaire. Because she could not understand Father, neither could I, and I was drawn into her unhappiness.

And yet that Christmas was one of our loveliest. All the decorations on the small tree were homemade. We still hang on our Christmas tree each year a small silver chain made of little beads of tinfoil, rolled from the paper in Father's packages of Sphinx cigarettes. We cut pictures out of the English illustrated magazines to replace the horrors on the wall which came with the rented villa. My presents were the very books I had asked for, plus colored pencils and a fresh box of watercolors and a new notebook with a marbleized cover. What we ate for Christmas dinner I don't remember; all we ate that winter, it seemed, was rabbit, which was plentiful and cheap; and Berthe, the eighteen-year-old girl Mother had brought with her from Publier (for, even that austere winter, she managed to have help), cooked rabbit every conceivable way. And a few inconceivable, Father would add. We also ate hearts of palm; for some reason the village grocer had an overabundance of this delicacy, and needed to unload it. Berthe bargained with him and came home triumphantly with string bags bulging with cans.

—*ML'E*

I was grateful at Christmastide to have time for these thoughts, away from the busy schedule which never seems to let up in the city. Here, at night, I can listen to the silence which is broken not by sirens and taxi horns but by the creaking of a house that is about two hundred and fifty years old. It was built by hardy folk. They didn't have the machinery we have to make things easier. Men and mules did the work. The wood for our house didn't come from a lumberyard, but from the great forest that surrounded the original village; it must have taken incredible strength to have felled the tree that is our roof beam.

And those who built had to be hardy spiritually as well as physically. The doors at Crosswicks are Cross-and-Bible doors. The hardware is HL—Help Lord—and they needed help. The weak survived neither the long, cold winters nor the heat of summer. Women and infants died in childbirth; grief was a daily companion, but it was also part of their spiritual life, their pattern of creation.

—*ML'E*

# PRESENTS

What's so good as getting?
The anticipation, snow
in the air, people with lists,
voices that drop when you
enter the room, the pine-wood
fire smell and the smell of pine
needles from the trimmed tree
by the window—it all narrows down
to the heft of the package in the
hands, the wondering, the unwrapping
(Careful—the paper's too pretty
to tear), the Oh, the Ah. What's
so good as getting

if not giving?
The covert questions, the catalogs
with corners turned back, the love
that overlooks cost, the hiding place
in the hamper, the card whose
colored words can't say it all,
the glee of linking want/wish
with have/hold, the handing over,
fingers brushing, the thing
revealed, the spark as the eyes
meet, and the hug. What's
as good as giving?

Christmas is the time of gifts. But have you noticed how much the advertising of consumer goods plays on our most selfish and materialistic impulses? Rather than being told to give generously to others, we hear "Be good to yourself," "Live a little," "You *deserve* it!" By such maxims we all too easily rationalize our own Yuletide self-indulgence.

In a "give me" age, things that once had to be earned are now expected as "our rights." People, once honored and valued, are taken for granted. Selfism has become the new idolatry, and "I'm *worth* it" the new rule of thumb. Material values have risen to the top rung of the ladder, and anything we cannot see and touch and prove and *use* is discounted as irrelevant; spiritual realities are dismissed as impractical and insignificant in an age of upward mobility.

How refreshing it is, in this context, to think of the downward mobility of Jesus, who left behind the riches of heaven, stripped himself of kingly splendor, was willing to be as poor and abused and out of step with his age as the most threadbare beggar he reached down and touched with the gift of love and healing. Jesus said, "It is better to give than to receive," and proved that he meant it when he gave his life away to us.

—LS

## WHAT HAVE WE DONE TO CHRISTMAS?

Christmas! God, leaving power and glory and coming to live with us, powerless, human, mortal. What have we done to Christmas?

—ML'E

# TREE AT CHRISTMAS

The children say the tree must reach the ceiling,
And so it does, angel on topmost branch,
Candy canes and golden globes and silver chains,
Trumpets that toot, and birds with feathered tails.
Each year we say, each year we fully mean:
"This is the loveliest tree of all." This tree
Bedecked with love and tinsel reaches heaven.
A pagan throwback may have brought it here
Into our room, and yet these decked-out boughs
Can represent those other trees, the one
Through which we fell in pride, when Eve forgot
That freedom is man's freedom to obey
And to adore, not to replace the light
With disobedient darkness and self-will.
On Twelfth Night when we strip the tree
And see its branches bare and winter cold
Outside the comfortable room, the tree
Is then the tree on which all darkness hanged,
Completing the betrayal that began
With that first stolen fruit. And then, O God,
This is the tree that Simon bore uphill,
This is the tree that held all love and life.
Forgive us, Lord, forgive us for that tree.
But now, still decked, bedecked, in joy arrayed
For these great days of Christmas thanks and song.
This is the tree that lights our faltering way,
For when man's first and proud rebellious act
Had reached its nadir on that hill of skulls
These shining, glimmering boughs remind us that
The knowledge that we stole was freely given
And we were sent the spirit's radiant strength
That we might know all things. We grasp for truth
And lose it till it comes to us by love.
The glory of Lebanon shines on this Christmas tree,
The tree of life that opens wide the gates.

The children say the tree must reach the ceiling,
And so it does: for me the tree has grown so high
It pierces through the vast and star-filled sky.

—*ML'E*

# EVER GREEN

topped
with an earth-bound angel
burdened
with man-made stars
tinsel bound
but touched with
no true gold
cropped
girdled with electricity
why be
a temporary tree
glass-fruited
dry
de-rooted?

when you may be
planted with purpose
in a flowered field
and where
living in clean light
strong air
crowned with the repeated gold
of every evening,
every night
real stars may nest
in your elbow
rest
be found in your shade
healing
in your perennial green
and from deep springs your roots
may suck enough to swell
your nine sweet fruits.

—LS

Cribb'd, cabined, and confined within the contours of a human infant. The infinite defined by the finite? The Creator of all life thirsty and abandoned? Why would he do such a thing? Aren't there easier and better ways for God to redeem his fallen creatures?

And what good did it all do? The heart of man is still evil. Wars grow more terrible with each generation. The earth daily becomes more depleted by human greed. God came to save us and we thank him by producing bigger and better battlefields and slums and insane asylums.

And yet Christmas is still for me a time of hope, of hope for the courage to love and accept love, a time when I can forget that my Christology is extremely shaky and can rejoice in God's love through love of family and friends.

*—ML'E*

Jesus Evergreen, from top to toe
your springy boughs are hung
with surprise—a gift here, a gift
there—wreathed with a glitter
of graces, all your needles
lacy with air and the remembrance
of small snow, your freshness
filling the house with the festal
smell of the forest. Your tough
length has bent to the wind, the axe,
but now the centering trunk
lances straight up, piercing
your slow green dying with the ache
of being felled. While the rooted
mountain spruces sing, resin
bleeds from your cut heart.

—LS

# Miracle on 10th Street

snapshot of a little girl, a piano, a Christmas tree. What could be more ordinary, more normal, more safe? But it wasn't safe that Christmas. It might have been ordinary and normal, because what happened to us happens to many people, but it wasn't safe!

This little girl, our first child, is looking wistfully at the tree, and her usual expression was vital, mischievous, full of life. But that Christmas she was wilted, like a flower left too long without water. She sat with her toy telephone and had long, quiet conversations with her lion ("You can never talk while the lion is busy," she would explain). She didn't run when we took her to the park. She was not hungry. I bathed her and felt her body, and there were swollen glands in her groin, her armpits.

We took her to the doctor. He looked over our heads and used big medical words. I stopped him. "What you are saying is that you think she has leukemia, isn't it?" Suddenly he looked us in the eye. When he knew that we knew what he feared, he treated us with compassion and concern. We knew the symptoms because the child of a friend of ours had died of leukemia. We knew.

We took our little girl to the hospital for tests, and she was so brave that her very gallantry brought tears to my eyes. We went home to our small apartment and sat in the big chair and told stories and knew that we would have several days' wait for the test results because of the holidays.

My husband was an actor. I am a writer. Like most artists, we had vivid imaginations. We tried hard not to project into the unknown future, to live right where we were, in a small apartment on 10th Street in New York City. We loved our apartment, where we slept on a couch in the living room. To get to the bedroom we had to walk through the kitchen and then the bathroom. At that time Leonard Bernstein lived on the top floor and would occasionally knock on our door to leave his suitcases when he did not want the long climb up the stairs. We were happy. My husband was playing on Broadway. I had had two books published and was working on a third. We had a beautiful child.

And suddenly the foundations rocked beneath us. We understood tragedy and that no one is immune. We remembered a church in New England where, carved in the wood of the lintel, are the words: REMEMBER, NO IS AN ANSWER.

My mother grew up in a world of Bible stories, and I thought of the marvelous story of Shadrach, Meshach, and Abednego. These three young men refused to bow down to an idol, a golden image, and King Nebuchadnezzar was so furious that he ordered them to be thrown into a furnace so hot that the soldiers who threw them into the fire were killed by the heat.

But Shadrach, Meshach, and Abednego stood there in the flames, unhurt, and sang a song of praise of all creation.

King Nebuchadnezzar was astonished and asked, "Did we not cast three men bound into the fire?" They answered, "True, O King." He replied, "But I see four men loose, walking in the midst of the fire, and they are not hurt, and the appearance of the fourth is like the Son of God."

And that, perhaps, is the most astounding part of the whole story. God did not take Shadrach, Meshach, and Abednego out of the fiery furnace. God was in the flames with them.

Yes, it is a marvelous story, but I thought, *I am not Shadrach, Meshach, or Abednego and the flames burn.*

I rocked my child and told her stories and prayed incoherent prayers. We turned on the lights of the Christmas tree, lit a fire in our fireplace, turned out all the other lights, and I managed to sing lullabies without letting my voice break, or tears flow. When my husband got home from the theater we put her to bed, and we held each other. We knew that the promise has never been safety, or that bad things would not happen if we were good and virtuous. The promise is only that God is in it with us, no matter what it is.

Even before the test results came from the hospital our little girl began to revive, to laugh, to wriggle as we sat together on the piano bench to sing carols. Our hearts began to lift as we saw full life returning to her, and the tests when they were returned indicated that she had had an infection. It was not leukemia. She was going to be all right. She is now a beautiful young woman with children of her own, and she has gone through her own moments of terror when her eldest child was almost killed by a car. I suspect that most parents know these times. I know that the outcome is not always the one we pray for. In my own life there have been times when the answer has indeed been NO. My husband died, and I will miss him forever. This past July 28 the car I was in was hit by a truck and I was almost killed. I am still recuperating and wondering by what miracle my life was saved, and for what purpose. Certainly everything is more poignant. Were the autumn leaves this year more radiant than usual? What about the tiny new moon I saw last night? And my family and my friends: Have I ever loved them as much as I love them now?

I think back to that Christmas when my husband and I did not know whether our little girl would live to grow up.

Between that Christmas and this there have been many times when I have been in the fiery furnace, but I am beginning to understand who is in there with me and that when I need it, I am given courage I never knew I had. Every day is a miracle, and I hope that is something I will never forget.

—ML'E

# "ANESTHETICS"

**O**ur youngest child, when he first became conscious of vocabulary, often did violence to words in absurd little ways which delighted us. Hugh and I listened seriously, lest we make him self-conscious or think we were laughing at him. We needn't have worried; he plunged into vocabulary like a sea gull into water, entirely fascinated with whatever he came up with. Even the laughter of his elder siblings did not deter him, and he is now happily malapropping in Latin, French, and German. One day, aged seven, he came home from school highly indignant because the boys' gym period had been curtailed. "We only had ten minutes of gym," he said, "and that was all anesthetics."

This was not just something to laugh at; it sent me back to my own, dreaded gym periods where anesthetics rather than calisthenics would have been more than welcome. Any team I was on lost automatically; when teams were chosen, mine was the last name to be reluctantly called out, and the team which had the bad luck to get me let out uninhibited groans. I now have this emotion at my fingertips if I need it for a story I'm writing; or if I need it to comfort some child who is going through a similar experience. It does us good to listen to things differently.

I remember "anesthetics" not only because it reminded me of my own pains over gym but because this small, delectable laugh came while I was in the middle of a very bad period, literarily speaking, and needed any reason for laughter, no matter how trivial. *A Wrinkle in Time* was on its long search for a publisher. Finally one, who had kept the manuscript for three months, turned it down on the Monday before Christmas. I remember sitting on the foot of our bed, tying up Christmas presents, and feeling cold and numb: anesthetized. I was congratulating myself on being controlled and grownup, and found out only later that I'd made a mess of the Christmas presents; I'd sent some heady perfume to a confirmed bachelor, and a sober necktie to a sixteen-year-old girl. So I called Theron, my agent: "Send the manuscript back to me. Nobody's ever going to take it, it's too peculiar, and it just isn't fair to the family." He didn't want to send it back, but I was cold and stubborn, and finally he gave in.

My mother was with us for the holidays, and shortly after Christmas I had a small party for her with some of her old friends. One of them, Hester Stover, more than ever dear to me now, said, "Madeleine, you must meet my friend, John Farrar." I made some kind of disgruntled noise, because I never wanted to see another publisher; I was back to thinking I ought to learn to bake cherry pie. But Hester, going to a good deal of trouble, insisted on setting up an appointment, and I took the subway down to John Farrar's office. I just happened to have that rather bulky manuscript under my arm.

He couldn't have been kinder or warmer. He knew some of my other work and was generous enough to say that he liked it, and he asked me what I was up to now. I explained that I had a book that I kind of liked, but nobody else did, or if they did, they were afraid of it.

I left it with him. Within two weeks I was having lunch with him and Hal Vursell, and signing a contract. "But don't be disappointed if it doesn't do well," they told me. "We're publishing it because we love it."

It is a right and proper Cinderella story. And I'm sure Cinderella appreciated her ball gown more because she'd been forced to sit by the ashes in rags for a long time before her fairy godmother arrived.

—ML'E

# THE MEANING OF CHRISTMAS TREES

It is light that tugs
that teaches each
grounded cone seed
to defy the pull
down, to interrupt air
space. And falling,
filtering through
the needles
it is rain that rises,
then, like a spring
at a sapling's heart.
It is the north wind
that trains, toughens
the white pine wood.
It is time that spreads
the grain in rings,
dark ripples in a
slow pond.

The pines learn slowly,
well. Up, around
and out they twist,
finding the new directions
of the old spiral
branded in each branch,
compacting, a wood
good enough for men
to craft into a crib
for a newborn, a cross
for pain, a plain table
for bread and wine, a door
for daylight.

—LS

# FALLING INTO SENTIMENTALITY

I love the Christmas tree with the family gathering together to decorate it, but I wish that we were like the French (and many others) who do their gift-giving on Epiphany, with the coming of the Wise Men, and keep Christmas Day itself as a holy day. We forget the holiness and fall into sentimentality over the tiny baby in the stable. Who is that tiny baby? Even the Creator, almighty and terrible and incomprehensible!

—*ML'E*

## CIRCLED WITH LIGHT

Our house is open, Lord, to Thee.
Come in, and share our Christmas tree!

We've made each nook and corner bright,
Circled with Christmas candle-light.

But light that never burns away
Is found in Thee alone, Lord. Stay,

Shine in us now, our Christmas Cheer,
And fill each niche of our New Year.

—*LS*

CHAPTER 6

# Our Morning Star

*Epiphany*

# The Eve of Epiphany

When I was a little girl in France I put out my shoes on the Eve of Epiphany. They were only ordinary shoes, not proper sabots, so I wasn't sure that they would be noticed by the three Wise Men; but in the morning one shoe held a new drawing pad, and the other a box of colored pencils. I like the idea of presents and feasting on Twelfth Night, so that Christmas can follow quietly on Advent. Christmas doesn't start until Christmas Eve, and then it can go on and on and the tree shines as brightly on Epiphany as on Christmas Day.

And there's more time to make things, which is one of the joys of Christmas. Our favorite presents are the homemade ones. Several years ago we decided that we were not going to be bullied by the post office or the Greeting Card Establishment into mailing our cards well before Christmas. We make our own cards, and I may not get an idea for one well before Christmas, for one thing. And there are a goodly number of people we write to only once a year, tucking the letter in with the card. So for the past several years we've taken our time, and as long as the last Christmas letter gets mailed before Lent, that's all I worry about, and Epiphany is a season of joy instead of exhaustion.

*Epiphany*

*Unclench your fists*
*Hold out your hands.*
*Take mine.*
*Let us hold each other.*
*Thus is his Glory*
*Manifest.*

God became man, was born of a woman, and we would have liked to keep this man-child with us forever; and that kind of possessiveness leads to disaster; as most parents know.

When I wrote the following lines I thought of them as being

in Mary's voice, but they might just as well be in mine—or any parent's.

*Now we may love the child.*
*Now he is ours,*
*this tiny thing,*
*utterly vulnerable and dependent*
*on the circle of our love.*
*Now we may hold him,*
*feeling with gentle hands*
*the perfection of his tender skin*
*from the soft crown of his head*
*to the sweet soles of his merrily kicking feet.*
*His fingers softly curl*
*around one finger of the grownup hand.*
*Now we may hold.*
*Now may I feel his hungry sucking at my breast*
*as I give him my own life.*
*Now may my husband toss him in the air*
*and catch him in his sure and steady hands*
*laughing with laughter as quick and pure*
*as the baby's own.*
*Now may I rock him softly to his sleep,*
*rock and sing,*
*sing and hold,*
*This moment of time is here,*
*has happened, is:*
*rejoice!*

*Child,*
*give me the courage*
*for the time*
*when I must open my arms*
*and let you go.*

I looked at my last baby lying in his cradle, knowing that he was the last child I would bear, for I nearly didn't survive his birth;

looked, touched, listened, with an incredible awareness I might not have had if I had been able to expect to bear more children. As each change came, I had to let the infant-that-was go, go forever. When he was seven months old I weaned him, as part of that essential letting go, letting him move on to child, little boy, young man. . . . Love, and let go. Love, and let go.

—*ML'E*

# Epiphany

hen a real epiphany comes for me, I recognize it as God dealing with me in a direct, irrefutable way. One such sighting came in the fall of 1988. I was teaching poetry at Regent College in Vancouver, Canada, while living an hour away, in Bellingham, Washington.

The Pacific Northwest is known for its rains that fall steadily for days (or weeks) and for clouds that hug the earth, shrouding the landscape in a gentle gloom. Just a few miles in from the coast rise the Cascade Mountains and, spectacular among them, Mt. Baker.

I wrote in my journal:

> *For weeks I've driven my highway, north in the morning, then south again at the end of the day. The mountains are clearly marked on the map, but they might as well not exist, lost as they are in clouds, obscured by drizzle, fog, haze. Then, some morning, unexpectedly, a strong air from the sea will lick away the fog and allow the sun to shine cleanly. And Mt. Baker, towering magnificently beyond the foothills, unbelievably high above the other mountains, is seen to be*

*what it has been all along—immense, serene, unmovable, its dazzling, snow-draped profile cut clear against a sky of jewel blue.*

*Today it happened. The mountain "came out"! I kept turning my eyes from the highway to look once more at its splendor, wanting to be overwhelmed again and again. It is heart-stopping. I can't get enough of it. And I can never take it for granted—I may not see it again for weeks.*

*It's God, showing me a metaphor of himself. I mean—he's there, whether I see him or not. It's almost as if he's lying in wait to surprise me. And the wind is like the Spirit, sweeping away my foggy doubt, opening my eyes, revealing the reality of God. Annie Dillard's words say it for me: "It was less like seeing than being for the first time seen, knocked breathless by a powerful glance. . . ."*

The word *epiphany* means, literally, *a showing*. Traditionally, this showing is accompanied by light; we need light in order to see what is being shown us. And light is something that every human heart longs for and responds to. Day holds all the clarity of brilliance and vision—a certainty, where night brings blindness in the unknowing dark.

Jesus himself was personified as the Sun of Righteousness. Even in our diurnal rhythms, day/night/day, sunset is a figure of chill, aging and death, while the appearance of the morning sun over the horizon's blackness speaks of warm hope, and a new beginning. This response is so universal that when God explains himself to us in Scripture as light—the "true Light that lightens everyone"—we recognize the glory and joy of the image.

In liturgical churches, the Feast of Epiphany is the first feast in the calendar New Year. Traditionally it falls on January 6 and celebrates the "showing" of the infant Christ to the Eastern sages in Bethlehem, where they had been led, curiously enough, by a star—a small, glowing, celestial flashlight for their dark path from the Orient. The star of Bethlehem is to me a remote spark from the universal Light toward whom the Wise Men were traveling, a coal from the blaze that sprang up when God struck his match in the world.

This event—the manifestation of Jesus to the Wise Men—is the sighting of God in the flesh, an event the church has seized upon that lights up the first week of our dark, wintry New Year. But it is not the only one. Often, at the most unexpected moments, Scripture—and life—bring into our focus other sets of sightings, or epiphanies. Perhaps every miracle that Jesus did, every healing, every teaching, was a new showing of himself.

Jesus said, "Blessed are the pure in heart, for they shall see God." This means that as humans are purged and rinsed clean, as they grow more transparent, so that their souls are like windows, they are invited into deeper seeings of God, appearings that have often been terrible—that is, full of terror. Think of Moses on Sinai, of Daniel in Babylon, or of John on Patmos confronted with the blazing glory of the One like the Son of Man. Think of the series of fearsome sightings in the early chapters of the Gospel of Luke, when the admonition "Don't be afraid" was an assurance badly needed by each of those confronted with a heavenly visitation—Zechariah, Mary, the shepherds.

Though the sudden, dazzling presence of God has often seemed a fearful thing for the humans involved, it has always been what I most dearly long for. God has sometimes disclosed himself to me in ways that I can only call indirect, through metaphors from life and nature and the Bible, through moments with a sense of significance about them, when everything suddenly danced into place. The inexplicable exhilaration of those rare instants redeemed, for a time, my days of chaos and confusion.

It's not difficult to remember or experience, with our baptized intellects or imaginations, times of new understanding *about* the Almighty. The Bible is full of metaphors that reveal God in images such as a rock, a banner, a mother hen, a lover, an artist. But all too often I have felt "in the dark" about God himself— unable to see *him*. Even though Jesus came close to us in the Incarnation, it all seems so long ago. I long for the immediate, unmistakable knowledge of his presence now, the smell, the sight, the touch of him. Even though its heat and light might scorch me, such "hard evidence" wouldn't be too hard for me to take.

I have often felt like the three disciples climbing down from Mount Tabor after the Transfiguration, unable to see ahead through the mist that covered the mountain after Jesus appeared to them. Sometimes, in the days following my husband's death, when life was very dark indeed, other people would come to me with stories of their dreams or visions of Harold, which seemed to them like epiphanies. Paula D'Arcy "saw" him among the worshipers on her church balcony on All Saints Day, "beaming with light and joy," as she expressed it to me in a phone call.

My friend Georgia Bosch dreamed that she and her husband were dining at our house, and after helping me in the kitchen she re-entered the dining room to see Harold sitting at the head of the table. "Luci thinks she's all alone," he told her, "but I'm watching, and I know everything she does." Margaret Smith has often *heard* God's plans and purposes for me in prayer. These were comforting assurances, but at a remove, circuitous, second-hand, not direct enough to satisfy me. Why didn't the Lord give *me* a vision? Why couldn't I, in the mountaintop sun with Peter, James, and John, see Jesus with his face shining "like the sun, and his clothes dazzling white as light"?

Both by nature and definition, epiphanies of the divine are rare. Exceptional. That is the way we recognize them for what they are. Like miracles, they are not part of the normal fabric of our lives. And they are nearly always individual rather than corporate experiences, personal rather than public spectacles. We cannot participate in the angel's announcement of the Incarnation to Mary except in imagination. Paul, going to Damascus, was felled to the ground when the flash of light from heaven surrounded him. But those traveling with him saw nothing. And when someone today tells us of their supernatural revelation from God, we cannot enter into it except by a faint, cognitive stirring.

I wonder if you will feel that stirring as I tell you about a Tuesday morning that same fall at Regent College when God made himself known to me even more unmistakably. Dr. James Houston came into my office, sat down, and said, almost without preamble, "I know that often in your life you have felt abandoned—by a father who was away preaching most of the time, by uncaring friends, now by Harold, whose death has left you alone, and by God. I believe that you will only find an answer to your sense of abandonment in *self-abandonment,* in willingness to give away to God your self, your identity. You've been walking through a long, black tunnel. Soon you will see light ahead of you, and when you come out of the tunnel you'll find yourself on the edge of a cliff. *You must throw yourself off the cliff edge and trust that God will catch you in his arms."* Startling words. They made me shiver because I had indeed felt the chill of that abandonment. But they also brought me the tingle of anticipation. I knew I needed to take this wise friend's words seriously. I needed to think through all the implications of his message from God to me, with its prophetic ring, so that I would know *how* to throw myself off the cliff.

The word Jim had used, "abandon," appealed to me. All my life I'd been urged by spiritual leaders to "yield," to "surrender" to God, to "relinquish" my idols. Through overuse those words had lost their impact and freshness for me, but the wildness, the impulsiveness of the word *abandon* challenged me to take this new risk.

On Tuesdays, people at Regent meet in small groups to pray and grow together in friendship. Journal in hand, I went to my car with Laurie, a young mother, her baby, and the baby's stroller, which I had to load into the trunk. We drove to the home where our group met, and when I got there I realized, with a sick jolt of panic, that the journal was gone.

Frantic, I rushed back to the campus in the car and checked in my office, then followed my cold trail through the building and out again to the parking lot. No journal. As I walked back to my car in the rain, I felt the interior tremor, the recognition of what this event really meant. My journal is an extension of me, as important as arm or leg. In it I feel my life condensed, myself embodied: my most personal observations and ideas and reflections are expressed and recorded in it in a way intensely valuable to me as a tracking of my life. I could buy another new, blank journal and start in again to reflect on its pages, but to lose this one, three-quarters full, was like losing myself. *Losing my self* . . . Suddenly I knew what was happening—God was pressing in for my gift. He was telling me the *how* of abandonment.

I gulped, then found myself saying, inwardly, *This is almost too painful to contemplate, but yes, if my journal stands for what you want from me, I'll give it up to you. I'll abandon it, and throw myself off the cliff edge. But oh, please be there to catch me!*

Still shaking, I drove back to the prayer group. As I pushed open the front door, Laurie met me and said, beaming, "Karen Cooper just phoned to say she'd found your journal in a puddle in the middle of University Avenue. You can pick it up at her house this afternoon." I realized that as I drove away from Regent it must have fallen off the top of the car, where I'd put it while stowing the stroller in the trunk.

Later, when Karen, my student and friend, handed the soggy journal back to me, there was a tire print stippled across its familiar, ugly, orange front cover; its back cover was half ripped off; and the coiled binding of its spine was bent and flattened. But it had been given back to me. I had made the jump. God had made the catch.

Karen and I prayed our exhilaration and thanks. She wondered aloud to me: "And some people doubt the personal involvement of God in their lives? Why should I, who knew you so well, and knew where to call you, be the one to stop my car in the rain, to find out what it was that had caught my eye, lying in that puddle? Why did I stop at all? Traffic was heavy. There were scores of cars and bicycles and pedestrians traveling on that busy street. But I found the journal and saw your name was written on the front."

In the same journal that night I wrote the story, and its conclusion:

> *If I am willing to abandon my will to God, broken like the spine of this journal, imprinted with God's own tire-track signature, he will give it back, and my identity with it. Oh, I feel it so profoundly, pierced to the core with its reality.*

*God does care for me. He has not abandoned me. I have been "knocked breathless by his powerful glance." He showed himself, beaming his light to my heart in a true epiphany.*

—*LS*

# THE DIVINE CHIAROSCURO

Epiphany, the showing of light, the revelation—perhaps its very evanescence is what lends it its appeal; if our days were routinely sun-filled, peaceful, tranquil, predictable, without conflict, their very serenity would soon seem flat, humdrum, and stale. God allows his brilliance to be highlighted by shadow and his summer warmth to be contrasted with winter chill so that we will know the difference and appreciate the light and warmth. There is purpose in the divine chiaroscuro.

—*LS*

# THE FIRST COMING

He came
    throwing off glory
    like fiery suns,
    leaving power behind,
    leaving the storms of hydrogen clouds,
    the still-forming galaxies,
    totally vulnerable
    as he emptied himself.

She took him in—
    into the deepest part of her being;
    she contained the tiny Word,
    smaller than the smallest
    subatomic particle,
    growing slowly
    from immortality into mortality,
    mother and child
    together in the greatest act of love
    the Maker could give the made.

Together they created
    immortality from mortality
    How? His father was Who?

He looked like any child
    from the vulnerable top
    of his tiny skull
    to the little curling toes.

This whispered Word made
    the sun and stars,
    wind and water,
    planets and moons, and all of us.
    But he left this joy
    to be

God With Us!
    understanding lowly shepherds

and two old people in the Temple.
Later, three wise men—
one from each human race—
came, pondering.
Most of the powerful people
were skeptical at best
God become Son of Man? Nonsense.

Christ will come,
expected or unexpected,
when God is ready,
even while we are loudly demanding
signs and proofs
which close our hearts and minds
to the Wildness of Love.

Word of Love,
enter our hearts
as you entered the virgin's womb.
Come, Lord Jesus!

—ML'E

## THE ARRIVAL OF LIGHT

I saw the sun coming up behind a tangle of trees. Most of the landscape was still in shadow, but where St. Charles Road merges with North Avenue, a round mouth of light opened—the sun shining through the throat of the road there, then looping toward me down a single telephone line. It was epiphany—the arrival of light—but so brief, so fleeting.

—LS

144

# IMAGES OF ICE

I stopped the car on impulse, left it parked on the gravel shoulder, and dove impulsively with camera into the prickly, thickly-bristling elderberry undergrowth just southeast of Van Kampen's brook.

An unseasonably warm rain the night before had been stopped in its tracks by a sudden cold wave so that everything flowing, running free, was swiftly solidified as by the wand of the White Witch of Narnia.

Through all the sloping woods bordering the road the small creeks and streams formed by the torrent of rain had been drowning the layered, copper-brown leaves. With the cold—temperatures plummeting from a mild sixty-five degrees to ten below—the swirls and eddies of water froze so fast that their lovely, abstract lines and curves are now perfectly preserved. My camera caught the leaves embedded in crystal or lifted on crests of paralyzed rainwater. When the air seeps under ice, its shape shows white, so that every bubble and ripple is outlined and highlighted. The thin skin of baroque ice, from which the water has now drained away, created a sculpture striking as Orrefors lead crystal.

The air is so still and sunny, with the ping of frost still in it, but I know how impermanent ice can be, like joy, like health, like life. Even if it warms up tomorrow, though, the images of ice will stay frozen on my film and I can repeat this moment of wonder, this epiphany, whenever I wish, as I look at my slides.

—*LS*

# STAR SONG

We have been having
epiphanies, like suns,
all this year long.
And now, at its close
when the planets
are shining through frost,
light runs
like music in the bones,
and the heart keeps rising
at the sound of any song.
An old magic flows
in the silver calling
of a bell,
rounding
high and clear,
flying, falling,
sounding
the death knell
of our old year,
the new appearing
of Christ, our Morning Star.

Now burst!
all our bell throats.
Toll!
every clapper tongue.
Stun the still night!
Jesus himself gleams through
our high heart notes
(it is no fable).
It is he whose light
glistens in each song sung
and in the true
coming together again
to the stable,
of all of us: shepherds,

sages, his women and men,
common and faithful,
wealthy and wise,
with carillon hearts
and, suddenly,
stars in our eyes.

—LS

# MAKING WORLDS:
## A CHILD'S PRAYER

Lord God,
you took great big handfuls of
chaos and made galaxies
and stars and solar systems
and night and day and sun and rain and snow
and me.
I take paint and crayon and paper
and make worlds, too,
along with you.

—ML'E

One time, when I was little more than a baby, I was taken to visit my grandmother, who was living in a cottage on a nearly uninhabited stretch of beach in northern Florida. All I remember of this visit is being picked up from my crib in what seemed the middle of the night and carried from my bedroom and out of doors, where I had my first look at the stars.

It must have been an unusually clear and beautiful night for someone to have said, "Let's wake the baby and show her the stars." The night sky, the constant rolling of breakers against the shore, the stupendous light of the stars, all made an indelible impression on me. I was intuitively aware not only of a beauty I had never seen before but also that the world was far greater than the protected limits of the small child's world which was all that I had known thus far. I had a total, if not very conscious, moment of revelation; I saw creation bursting the bounds of daily restriction, and stretching out from dimension to dimension, beyond any human comprehension.

This early experience was freeing, rather than daunting, and since it was the first, it has been the foundation for all other such glimpses of glory. And it is probably why the sound of the ocean and the sight of the stars give me more healing, more whole-ing, than anything else.

I turn again to the night sky, this time to a planet, one of the planets in our own solar system, the planet Mercury. Mercury revolves around our mutual parent sun in such a way that one face is always turned toward the sun and is brilliantly lit and burningly hot; and the other side is always turned toward the cold dark of interstellar space. But Mercury oscillates slightly on its axis, and thereby sunside and nightside are integrated by a temperate zone which knows both heat and cold, light and dark. So the two disparate sides of Mercury are not separated by a chasm; the temperate zone mediates.

Where, in ourselves, can we find this temperate zone which will integrate and free us? The words *freedom* and *liberation* have been used frequently during the last decade, and this would certainly seem to imply that we are less free, less liberated, than we want to admit. People who are already free don't need to talk about liberation. It is a great mistake to equate freedom with anarchy, liberation with chaos. It has been my experience that freedom comes as the temperate zone integrates sunside and nightside, thereby making wholeness instead of brokenness.

*—ML'E*


## An Icon of Creation

Stars have always been an icon of creation for me. During my high school years, when I was at my grandmother's beach cottage for vacations, I loved to lie on a sand dune and watch the stars come out over the ocean, often focusing on the brilliant grace of one particular star. Back in school, I wrote these lines:

> *I gaze upon the steady star*
> *That comes from where I cannot see,*
> *And something from that distant far*
>
> *Pierces the waiting core of me*
> *And fills me with an aweful pain*
> *That I must count not loss but gain.*
>
> *If something from infinity*
> *Can touch and strike my very soul,*
> *Does that which comes from out of me*
> *Reach and pierce its far off goal?*

Very young verses, but they contain the germ of an understanding of the interdependence of all Creation.

*—ML'E*

## THE FURTHEST REACHES
## OF TIME AND SPACE

My apartment faces west, and when I go to bed at night and turn out the lights I can see across the great Hudson River to the lights of New Jersey. I can often see the planes coming in, en route to La Guardia Airport, looking like moving stars, though even when the sky is clear there are few real stars visible because of the city lights that burn all night. I think of the nearest star, Proxima Centauri, about four light years away—about twenty-three million million miles. The rare stars I see may be three hundred light years away, and three thousand light years away, and three million. When we human creatures look up at the night sky we are able to see into the furthest reaches of time.

Not only time, but space—vast distances. Galaxies trillions of light years across. Suns so enormous that they make our own sun a mere pinprick.

—*ML'E*


## ATOMIC FURNACES

The morning star is low on the horizon. There are three more stars pulsing faintly in the city sky. But even if I can't see a skyful of stars they are there above me nevertheless; the Milky Way, our own galaxy, swings somewhere in the vast dark above the city lights.

All those stars. Suns. More suns than can be imagined. Great flaming brilliant atomic furnaces, the bursting of their atoms providing life. Providing life for their planets. Perhaps there are planets where that which was created by love returns love, and there is joy and worship and praise, and man sings with the angels.

—*ML'E*

## SOARING

When I think of the incredible, incomprehensible sweep of creation above me, I have the strange reaction of feeling fully alive. Rather than feeling lost and unimportant and meaningless, set against galaxies which go beyond the reach of the furthest telescopes, I feel that my life has meaning. Perhaps I should feel insignificant, but instead I feel a soaring in my heart that the God who could create all this—and out of nothing—can still count the hairs of my head.

—*ML'E*

## PERCEPTIONS: A JOURNAL ENTRY

It has been one of my perceptions this year that the beauty of Creation suffuses even decay and death—the *fallen* leaf, the fragile, *shattered* shell of ice, the *frozen* stream, the *burst* pod.

—*LS*

## WONDERFUL MIX OF CREATION

Christ, the second Person of the Trinity, has always been, is always, and always will be available to all people and at all times. We are so focused on the Incarnation, on Jesus of Nazareth, that sometimes we forget that the Second Person of the Trinity didn't just arrive two thousand years ago, but has always been. Christ was the Word that shouted all of Creation into being, all the galaxies and solar systems, all the subatomic particles, and the wonderful mix of Creation that is what makes up each one of us.

Jesus said, to the horror of the establishment people, *"Before Abraham was, I am."*

—*ML'E*

## AN OFFERING OF LOVE

Jesus should be for us the icon of icons, God sending heaven to earth, "Lord of Lords in human vesture." God has given us each other as revelations of divine creativity, and the ultimate revelation is in Jesus of Nazareth, the Incarnation of God into human flesh: *carne* = flesh. God enfleshed for our sakes. God's love offered to us fully and wonderfully and particularly in one person.

*—ML'E*

## THE ORDINARY SO EXTRAORDINARY

He came, quietly impossible,
Out of a young girl's womb,
A love as amazingly marvelous
As his bursting from the tomb.

This child was fully human,
This child was wholly God.
The hands of All Love fashioned him
Of mortal flesh and bone and blood,

The ordinary so extraordinary
The stars shook in the sky
As the Lord of all the universe
Was born to live, to love, to die.

He came, quietly impossible:
Nothing will ever be the same:
Jesus, the Light of every heart—
The God we know by Name.

*—ML'E*

# THE WISE MEN

A star has streaked the sky,
pulls us,
calls.
Where, oh where, where leads the light?

We came and left our gifts
and turned
homeward.
Time had passed, friends gone from sight—

One by one, they go, they die
to now,
to us—
gone in the dazzling dark of night.

Oh how, and where, and when, and why,
and what,
and who,
and may, and should, O God, and might

a star, a wind, a laugh, a cry
still come
from one—
the blazing word of power and might—

to use our gifts of gold and myrrh
and frankincense
as needed,
as our intention was to do the right?

Here, there, hear—soft as a sigh—
willing,
loving
all that is spoken, back to the flight

blazing too fierce for mortal eye.
Renew—
redeem,
oh, Love, until we, too, may dazzle bright.

—*ML'E*

# Royal Alchemy

piphany. "No longer do the magi bring presents to the moon and the stars, for this child made the moon and the stars."

These words were copied into my Goody Book (a big old "commonplace book" in which, for many years, I have copied out words that have stimulated and challenged me); I wrote down these words a long time ago, and where they came from or who wrote them I don't remember. Who were the magi? the magicians, the three wise men who came from far away to bring gifts to the child Jesus?

My bishop suggested that they were alchemists, and that when they brought their gifts they were giving Jesus their magic. Gold, frankincense, and myrrh are all part of the alchemical ingredients. At the time of this conversation, one of my granddaughters lent me a novel which had a lot in it about alchemy; what intrigued me especially was the suggestion that alchemists cared far more about reconciling male and female than they did about changing metal into gold.

Reconciling male and female: first, within ourselves, then, with each other. Perhaps this reconciliation was the priceless gift the magi gave to Jesus, along with the gold, frankincense and myrrh, and it was a much greater gift than the three tangible ones. Jesus accepted the gifts, and in turn gave the greatest of the gifts to

155

us. In a world where women were far less than second class citizens, he chose women for his closest friends—Mary of Magdala, Mary and Martha of Bethany. He spoke to a Samaritan woman at a well, breaking three taboos: men did not speak publicly to women, most certainly not to a Samaritan woman, and no good Jew would at that time have taken water from a Samaritan. Samaritans worshipped God differently from the Jews; they even worshipped on the wrong mountain. They were far more suspect than people from a different denomination. They did not belong. The woman at the well was awed by the gifts Jesus gave her, even the gift of loving acceptance. In her brokenness, she was able to receive the reconciliation of Jesus' healing.

In his living, his speaking, his action, Jesus offered the world the reconciliation the wise men had brought to him as their greatest gift and, alas, the world could not accept it then, and still, today, cannot. We are still part of that brokenness that split us asunder eons ago in the garden.

Is it not likely that if Adam and Eve had known how to wait, had trusted God's timing, that at the right moment God would have come to them? God would have come to them saying, "Here children, here is the fruit of the tree of knowledge of good and evil. You're ready for it. Eat."

But the serpent tempted them to be impatient, to break time, to rush into graduate school physics courses and depth psychology before they'd learned how to read.

Perhaps at the right moment God would have called Adam and Eve, saying, "The time has come for you to leave the safety of this beautiful garden where you have learned all that you can learn in this place. It is time for you to go out into the rest of the world." It would have been somewhat like the mother bird urging the fledglings out of the nest when they're ready to fly. But Adam and Eve weren't yet ready to fly, and we've been lumbering about on the ground ever since.

Of course that is a story, but it's a story that works for me, and one reason stories are icons for us human beings is that they are our best way of struggling to comprehend the incomprehensible. We do not know why our psyches are out of sync, but the story of Adam and Eve gives us creative glimpses.

When Descartes said, "I think, therefore I am," he did us no favor, but further fragmented us, making us limit ourselves to the cognitive at the expense of the imaginative and the intuitive. But each time we read the Gospels we are offered anew this healing reconciliation, and, if we will, we can accept the most wondrous gift of the magi.

My icon is the glory of the heavens at night, a cold, clear night when the stars are more brilliant than diamonds. The wise men looked at the stars, and what they saw called them away from their comfortable dwellings and towards Bethlehem. When I look at the stars I see God's glory in the wonder of creation.

The stars can become idols when we look to them for counsel, which should come only from God. For the magi, astronomy and astrology were one science, and it is probably a very sad thing that they ever became separated.

That is yet another schism which looks for healing, and we have not been as wise as the three magi who came from their far corners of the world, seeking the new King, the king who was merely a child. Surely if the world is as interdependent as the discoveries of particle physics imply, then what happens among the stars does make a difference to our daily lives. But the stars will not and should not tell us the future. They are not to be worshiped. Like the wise men, we no longer bring presents to the moon and the stars, for this Child made the moon and the stars. Alleluia!

—ML'E

I shall miss the stars.

Not that I shall stop looking
as they pattern their wild wills each night
across an inchoate sky, but I must see them with a different awe.
If I trace their flames' ascending and descending—
relationships and correspondences—
then I deny what they have just revealed.
The sum of their oppositions, juxtapositions,
led me to the end of all sums:
a long journey, cold, dark and uncertain,
toward the ultimate equation.
How can I understand? If I turn back from this,
compelled to seek all answers in the stars,
then this—Who—they have led me to
is not the One they said: they will have lied.
No stars are liars!
My life on their truth!
If they had lied about this
I could never trust their power again.

But I believe they showed the truth,
truth breathing,
truth Whom I have touched with my own hands,
worshipped with my gifts.
If I have bowed, made
obeisance to this final arithmetic,
I cannot ask the future from the stars without betraying
the One whom they have led me to.
It will be hard not to ask, just once again,
to see by mathematical forecast where he will grow,
where go, what kingdom conquer, what crown wear.
But would it not be going beyond truth
(the obscene *reductio ad absurdum*)
to lose my faith in truth once, and once for all
revealed in the full dayspring of the sun?

I cannot go back to night.
O Truth, O small and unexpected thing,
You have taken so much from me.
How can I bear wisdom's pain?
But I have been shown: and I have seen.

Yes. I shall miss the stars.

—*ML'E*

CHAPTER 7

# Newness
of
Heart

*New Year and*

*Late Winter*

# JOY

We are moving soberly towards the new year, joy for
an anguished world.

—*ML'E*

## FOR DANA

The end of the year is here. We are at a new
    beginning.
A birth has come, and we reenact
At its remembrance the extraordinary fact
Of our unique, incomprehensible being.

The new year has started, for moving and
    growing.
The child's laugh within and through the adult's
    tears,
In joy and incomprehension at the singing years
Pushes us into fresh life, new knowing.

Here at the end of the year comes the year's
    springing.
The falling and melting snow meet in the stream
That flows with living waters and cleanses the
    dream.
The reed bends and endures and sees the dove's
    winging.

Move into the year and the new time's turning
Open and vulnerable and loving and steady.
The stars are aflame; creation is ready.
The day is at hand: the bright sun burns.

—*ML'E*

163

# SAYING YES

One New Year's Eve I was allowed, for the first time, to stay up with my parents until midnight. I remember only one thing about that milestone: while the village clock was striking twelve, Father opened his small new engagement diary for the year, and we all signed our names in it. It was Father's way of saying *yes* to Mother and to me and to the new year, no matter what it might bring. It would have been much easier for him to withdraw from it, as he occasionally withdrew from the pain with whiskey, but he refused to withdraw, and I knew this without understanding it in the least, and was grateful as I added my signature to Mother's and his.

*—ML'E*

# THE COLLECTOR

In our house, the first of January
heralds a resolute simplicity. No,
not just the clean calendar on the
kitchen door, nor the new date
on letters; not even the bundling out
of the dry tree with its trail
of needles to the back porch,
but a return to routine. Clearing
the Christmas clutter
signals renewal, a re-ordering;
it is a woman taking off jewelry
before scrubbing the kitchen floor.

And so I lift away the mantel's
necklace, a cedar swag pointed with
blue berries and white lights.
Down comes the rosy ribbon from
the decoy duck's neck, the holly sprig
from the antique scale (my husband
was weighed on it when he was born),
the scarlet candles, riskily lop-
sided from all December's burnings.

For myself, and for this shelf
across the fire-place brick,
I plan a chasteness free of dust
and trivia—a candle-stick or two,
a copper bowl, paired pottery crocks
to anchor arcs of bittersweet.
But with a barely noticed stealth
the wooden width accumulates
its own decor: a spindrift of screws,
shipping labels, old lists,
a brass bell turned silent—its
clapper tongue plucked out by
the root, a pulled wishbone,

a curious knot of wood, an envelope
scribbled with verse, and in April,
part of a robin's egg chipped
from the sky. Disorder spreads
so surely along the mantelpiece
that by early June I feel as though
the only things I've failed
to keep there are
my New Year's resolutions.

—*LS*

# HOW TO PAINT
# A PROMISE IN JANUARY

*for Lauren*

Here in my winter breakfast room,
the colors of rainbows are
reduced to eight solid lozenges in a
white metal tray. A child's brush
muddies them to gray in a
glass of water. Even the light breaks down
as it pushes through the rain-streaked
windows and polishes the wooden table
imperfectly.
 Green leaves always turn
brown. Summer died into the dark days
a long time ago; it is hard even to
remember what it was like, stalled
as I am in this narrow slot of time
and daylight.
 Until I look down again
and see, puddling along the paper,
under a painted orange sun
primitive as the first spoked wheel,
the ribbon of color flowing out of
my grand-daughter's memory—a new
rainbow, arc-ing wet over strokes of grass
green enough to be true.

—LS

# Yes to Shame
# and Glory

t Christmas, most of us Protestants are tolerant enough to allow Mary limited access onto our greeting cards and into our crèches and carols. But the rest of the year she is a victim of simple neglect. In bending over backwards to avoid certain excesses of veneration, we have abandoned Mary to a kind of religious limbo.

Yet it could be different if we avoid both extremes, and look at Mary clearly enough to see the woman shown us in the Bible. Not only was she a simple mortal, unpretentious enough for us all to identify with, but she nudges our self-centered "me generation" toward the path of the God-centered, the faithful, the obedient. If we read Mary into each one of the Beatitudes, we will not falsify her character.

From Mary we may also learn about the courage to say yes, especially as we are faced with challenges from God that may seem to us nearly as impossible or outrageous as the angel's demand.

Mary said yes to God. Perhaps God chose her body and her spirit as the venue for Christ's arrival on our planet because he knew it was her habit of life to say yes to her father and her Father.

> *. . . We have seen the studies, sepia strokes*
> *across yellowed parchment, the fine detail*
> *of hand and breast and the fall of cloth—*
> *Michelangelo, Caravaggio, Titian, El Greco,*
> *Rouault—each complex madonna positioned,*
> *sketched, enlarged, each likeness plotted at last*
> *on canvas, layered with pigment, like the final*
> *draft of a poem after thirty-nine roughs.*
>
> *But Mary, virgin, had no sittings, no chance*
> *to pose her piety, no novitiate for body or*
> *for heart. The moment was on her unaware:*
> *the Angel in the room, the impossible demand,*
> *the response without reflection. Only one*
> *word of curiosity, echoing Zechariah's How?*
> *yet innocently voiced, without request for proof.*
> *The teen head tilted in light, the hand*
> *trembling a little at the throat, the candid*
> *eyes, wide with acquiescence to shame and*
> *  glory—*
> *"Be it unto me as you have said."*

After Mary said her unmistakable yes, after her insemination by the Spirit of God, "the angel left her" isolated, in silence. His bright presence had imprinted itself in her eyes, his words still sang in her ears, the seed of God burned in her body. No wonder she needed to talk to another woman! And how serendipitous it must have seemed that God had also worked a miracle of conception in Elizabeth.

Two Greek words for *blessed* give us significant clues to the kind of person Mary was. In chapter 1 of the Gospel of St. Luke, Elizabeth's greeting word is *eulogetos*—"Blessed are you among women"—a term that told her, as had Gabriel, that she was specially favored, or well-spoken of, by the Lord.

This Jewish blessing could not be revoked or reversed; the sound and the meaning of it would live and throb in Mary's mind as a perpetual sign of God's affirmation and approval, in spite of all the trials that would track her life. Being "blessed" meant that God favored and trusted her enough to burden her with one of life's most difficult roles: being the mother of a paradox—one who was God enfleshed in a man's body, yet one who was considered a failure and, ultimately, a criminal.

The other word for *blessed* used by Elizabeth was *makarios*—which means "satisfied, fulfilled, full of God." The context in which Elizabeth spoke this prophetic word was significant. Mary was to be full of God (both physically and spiritually) because she "believed that what the Lord had said to her would be accomplished." The Spirit-impelled dialogue between these two women occurs in a kind of euphoria of holy wonder. "My spirit rejoices in God my Savior!" Marvel! *Sing* aloud to the Lord! (Is she thinking and speaking, this pregnant adolescent, in italics and exclamation marks?)

It is almost too extraordinary for her to believe that, young and inexperienced and unremarkable and female as she is, through *her* Jehovah will "help his servant Israel."

Mary will need the exhilaration of these days to balance the pain of the next thirty-three years and beyond. For God's trust of her is deep enough not only to fill her with his heavy glory but also to draw her into the agony of Incarnation, to share with her the inevitable clash of spirit with flesh, of infinite with finite. There was as much pain as there was promise in that moment when Mary became a mother-to-be.

In the biblical account Mary seems more mother than wife. And like all human mothers, certainly like me with my children, Mary knew not only pride but pain. I think I'm like my son John, who as a young boy once asked me, "Why did God make me so I feel hurt so easily?" I thought a bit before I replied, "Because he knows that your capacity for beauty will only be as deep as your sensitivity to pain."

I wonder, sometimes, about young people today who choose to be childless. In their concern for career, comfort, convenience, for personal development, may they be depriving themselves of one of God's most effective teaching tools? Had I lived without the singing joy as well as the devastating pain of being a parent, my understanding and appreciation of God the Father would have been drastically limited.

Mary didn't close herself off from God in such a way; she said yes without knowing all that parenthood would involve, but with trust that God knew, and that he was the Parent who loved her.

Mary. Her name means bitterness. From the hour of Announcement on, dark pain lay ahead—friends' incredulity, lack of understanding, accusations of promiscuity and her son's illegitimacy, to begin with. She also faced the possible loss of her betrothed, Joseph; until the angel reversed his direction through a dream, Joseph had resolved to break the contract between them and leave Mary to carry and bear her baby alone.

After she had returned from Elizabeth to her own village, to make her home with Joseph, Mary experienced the weariness of months of pregnancy—an unsensational hardship, culminating in the long, southward journey from Nazareth to Bethlehem. She and Joseph were poor, and even if they had a donkey to ride, a blanket on the back of an ass is no easy seat for a woman nine months pregnant, her body cold and stiff from sitting on the plodding animal for hours at a time.

Bethlehem, in turn, seemed so harsh and unwelcoming in the winter night. Perhaps her first uneasy cramping of labor had begun, and the panic of helplessness as the busy innkeeper turned them away.

There is no indication in St. Luke's Gospel that the baby born so infelicitously to Mary is anything unusual—just another out-of-wedlock child born to a teenager on the road. It is the shepherds who receive the birth announcement who express amazement, who see and identify this newborn as someone unique. Talk about light shining out of darkness! Talk about paradox! That red, squashed baby face is the brightest thing a manger has ever contained.

Reading and meditating about Mary, I am reminded again and again of the juxtaposition of opposites that recur in the Bible. The pain of childbirth joined with the exhilaration of having produced the manchild who was God. The pain of place—an animal shelter humble and primitive—coupled with the glory of the shepherds' numinous experience: an affirmation of the miraculous, with angels at their work of announcement again. The excitement of the arrival of wealthy Gentile astrologers, bringing worship and exotic gifts to the feet of a Jewish baby, resulted later in the awful weight of pain that Mary must have felt at Herod's massacre of the infants. She realized that her own little one was protected at the life-cost of all the baby boys of Bethlehem who died in Jesus' place.

Joy and pain must have struggled for supremacy in Mary's emotions as she tried, in her soul's privacy, to put it all together, to weigh each event and wait for its meaning to come clear. If she had lived today, she might have caught it all in a journal, as I did during the recent months of my husband's illness and death. I learned, as Mary must have, that woven into the fabric of life crises are moments of epiphany and exultation. The paradox of God's plans! Mary, illiterate, had to hoard it all in her intelligent heart.

Mary's calling was to carry the body of God, and to bear not only her own pain but her son's, feeling his anguish as intensely as all mothers before or since have felt with their children.

As the Law dictated, Jesus' parents presented their new son to the Lord in the Jerusalem temple. Simeon's prophetic words, spoken out to God with God's own child cradled in his arms, glittered with golden words—peace, salvation, light, revelation, glory. But then, as the old man turned and fixed his piercing eyes on Mary, he uttered a blessing that was weighted with both promise and foreboding: "This child is destined to cause the falling and rising of many in Israel, and to be a sign that will be spoken against, so that the thoughts of many hearts will be revealed. And a sword will pierce your own soul too" (Gospel of Luke, NIV). With his soul's eyes, Simeon saw the link between

Christ's rejection and Mary's own anguish, and from then on, the sword of his remembered words pierced and penetrated her.

Mary said yes to God. Did she wonder, during the next thirty-odd years, why he had invaded her body and her life in such a shocking, unparalleled way, only to keep her waiting as her son's years passed in the mundane dailiness of a small-town carpentry business? And further down the road, what questions about God's purposes filled her mind as her Promised One headed for certain destruction at the hands of his opponents? Unfulfilled promise in a child is always painful for a human mother, especially when prolonged. Perhaps she needed that shocking first Announcement, those unforgettable memories, to keep her going, to rekindle her belief in his destiny.

As he moved into maturity, did Jesus cause his mother another kind of pain? The Lord kept some of his hardest sayings for Mary (but "blessed is she who is not scandalized in me"). Feel, if you are a parent, the tone and the impact on her of words that disclose a higher loyalty: "Why were you searching for me? Didn't you know I had to be in my father's house?" (Why be so unreasonable? Why search for a truant twelve-year-old? Why feel anxiety when the son given you by God turns up missing and you cannot find him for at least three days? Why be astonished when you hear him not only asking but answering the questions of the temple theologians?) Yet this crisis of losing and finding, Mary also "treasured in her heart" (St. Luke).

After this Jesus returned with Mary and Joseph to Nazareth where, according to St. Luke's Gospel, he "was obedient to them . . . and grew in wisdom and stature, and in favor with God and men." Such growth also includes establishing emotional independence from parents, an uneasy process in any family, but one that Jesus had already begun during the Jerusalem trip. It is painful for any mother to see her child need her nurture and protection less and less, and surely Mary was not immune to this pain.

Mary's womanly concern is demonstrated again at the wedding feast at Cana. When she alerts Jesus to the problem of the wine shortage, he seems to distance himself from it and her. "Why involve me?" he asks, and it sounds like a rebuke.

In the account given in St. Mark's Gospel of the family's visit to Jesus (he was tangling with the Jewish teachers of the law), Christ seems again to be pulling away from his mother and brothers. He has been accused of demon possession, of performing miracles by Satan's power, and even his kin are worried that he is "out of his mind." Yet when he is told that his concerned mother and brothers are outside looking for him, he counters with a rhetorical question, "Who are my mother and my brothers?" and then answers it. It is those seated in the circle around him. "Whoever does God's will is my brother and sister and mother." Blood relationships are discarded in favor of the larger family of God. For Mary, her heart already bearing the wounds of love, such words must have stung.

The culmination of Mary's pain and glory is shown in the final references to her in the nineteenth chapter of St. John's Gospel and in the first chapter of the Acts of the Apostles. At the cross, under its very arm, near its human victim, she waits in a trinity of Marys, and reading between the terse lines of Scripture we can guess at what she is going through. "Lord, here I am," that long-ago surrender, seems easy compared with "Lord, here is my son."

By now she has learned one of the lessons I am just beginning to understand—that pain is a fire that purges; that it works in us what no amount of pleasure can accomplish; that it is best not to dodge pain but to let it hurt, and to live through it to the other side. The games we play to distract ourselves or numb the pain only postpone its benefits.

Mary has reached the nadir of anguish. She has said yes to God and gone through all the allotted pain of his purpose for her. The next words in St. John's Passion narrative are full of a tenderness and love that transform pain. "When Jesus saw his mother there, with the disciple whom he loved standing nearby, he said to his mother, 'Dear woman, here is your son,' and to the disciple, 'Here is your mother.'"

After the resurrection and ascension of Jesus, Mary found her rightful place in the upper room with the others of his inner circle (as seen in the first chapter of Acts), equally joined with them in the risk and intimacy of prayer, the responsibility for the young church. By faithfulness she had demonstrated her value to God and to his "sent ones." Her suffering had been redemptive.

It took over thirty years—a long testing time for a human. But after the purging pain came the healing love and the rewards of glory: the filling with the breath of God at Pentecost, the tongues of fire, telling both heat and light. That is what happens when any of us says yes to God, as Mary did.

—LS

## JOYFUL IN THE NEWNESS OF THE HEART

*7 January 1979*

Joyful in the newness of the heart,
Astonished by love's blazing light,
Making an end to a new start,
Early to smile, swift & bright.
Singing His love, all night, all night.

Peace in the midst of chaos comes
Alert & lively, he's on the ready.
Remarkable, hearing different drums,
keeps open, & waiting, & steady.
Surely, surely the depths he plumbs

May the new year bring love, bring peace,
On the Close, the Cathedral, The loving heart
Ready for angels, looking for light,
Thinking of others, That pain may cease,
Often in prayer, by day, by night
Nurtured in love: may his joy increase!

—*ML'E*

During those weeks in Chamonix we went everywhere on skis, the simplest method of moving on the snow-packed streets, and I learned more complex skiing on the slopes above the villa. We spent a memorable day on the Mer de Glace, and those hours of walking over a sea of ice were a revelation of a cold and unearthly beauty I had never before seen. My own vision was deepened because I saw the beauty through the eyes of my parents; their wholehearted response took us all beyond the pain and confusion which were ever present in the villa. One night we rode for an hour in a horse-drawn sleigh, snow beneath us, moonlight and starlight above us, the horse's mane streaming coldly in the wind, while we were kept warm under fur robes. Father hardly coughed at all; Mother relaxed and enjoyed the beauty and the speed. I moved back into my dream world during that ride, not as an escape, but as a respite; I did not try to take the fairy tale with me back into the villa.

—*ML'E*

There is enough ground cover of snow to provide traction, and I have on good hiking boots. The dogs rush ahead, double back, rush ahead again. Once we are into the woods the wind drops and it is less cold. We get to the stone bridge over the brook, which is still running under its icy edges despite the subfreezing weather. To the right of the brook is the first and smaller of two remarkable beaver dams. We follow around the rim of the frozen pond to the larger dam, an amazing feat of engineering. The pond gleams silver. The winter light slants through the trees. We don't talk much, except to remark on some particular beauty or other—the light on the icicles near the first dam, a small bird's nest in a low cleft of a tree.

Then we tramp home to make cocoa and warm our toes. And think a little about the past year. There has been considerable personal grief. It has not been a good year for many of our friends. For the planet it has been an astounding year. The world events that shared the news with Hurricane Bob when I was first home from the hospital in San Diego have continued to accelerate. There is no more Soviet Union. The communist religion has gone down the drain with unprecedented rapidity. The bitter fighting between Serbs and Croats continues, the differences in religion making the fight more anguished.

What will happen in the next year is far from clear.

—*ML'E*

Instead of being allowed to grieve for the precariousness of all life, we are often taught to look for a security that does not exist. No one can promise that we will end a day in safety, that we, or someone dear to us, will not be hurt.

All too often we fall for it and go into debt to buy the latest gadget. Whatever it is, it's made to self-destruct after a few years, and it will never help whatever it is that's making us hurt.

What does help? The gift of Christ, who offers us the grieving that is healing. This kind of grieving is a gift; it helps us "Walk that lonesome valley." It involves a lifelong willingness to accept the gift, which is part of what Bonhoeffer called *costly grace.*

We were bought with a price, and what has cost God so much cannot be cheap for us.

The search for grace, costly grace, involves the acceptance of pain and the creative grief which accompanies growth into maturity. Don't be afraid the pain will destroy the wholeness. It leads, instead, to the kind of wholeness that rejoices in Resurrection.

We live in a time where costly grace is what makes life bearable; more than bearable—joyful and creative, so that even our grief is part of our partnership in co-creation with God.

The world around us is full of racial tension; the problems of starvation across the globe grow greater with each year; the planet is still torn apart by war; the result of our technocratic affluence is an earth depleted, an air polluted, and a population suffering from more mental illness, suicide, and despair than our country has ever known. So perhaps we finally have to accept that the great do-it-yourself dream hasn't worked, and we've been dreaming wrong, dreaming nightmares. The original dream had to do with a wholeness which touched every part of our lives, including grief, and it had to do with grace, costly grace.

—*ML'E*

# LIKE US

The petals on winter candles
grow from their seeds of light
up to a warmth that softens
the dark, hides the stain
on the sofa, kindles coals
in any eye
joined to their felicity.

They are time's victims
softened, like all of us,
by their own yellow heat,
uncertain in a wind,
annulled by lightning,
eating themselves toward
extinction (unless
their flickering ignites
new wicks behind
the eyelids of the mind.)

—LS

New Year's Eve and New Year's Day come not out of the church year but out of the dawn of human life. To our ancient forbears, many thousands of years before the birth of Jesus, the stretching nights of early winter and the shortening days were terrifying. Was the night going to swallow up the day? Was the life-giving sun going to slide down the western horizon and be lost forever? It must have seemed a real possibility to those dwellers in caves or tree houses, who knew nothing they could not see with their own eyes about the movements of the suns and the stars.

So, when it slowly became apparent that the sun was staying in the sky a minute longer than it had the day before, and then a minute longer, there was great rejoicing, and feasting and fun, and very likely (as today) too much fun. But it was more than fun. It was spontaneous gratitude that the world was not coming to an end.

In the story of the life of Jesus, the first day of January is marked as the feast of his circumcision. All good Jewish boys were ritually circumcised in the first ten days of their lives. So Joseph and Mary carried the eight-day-old baby to the temple and made the required offerings, *according to that which is said in the law of the Lord, a pair of turtle-doves or two young pigeons.* You might have thought that they would have had family and friends with them for this great event, but even in babyhood it seemed that Jesus turned things upside down. As far as we know there were only three witnesses: the high priest, a very old man named Simeon, and an equally old woman named Anna. Simeon believed that he would not die until he had seen the promised Messiah, and when the baby was put in his arms, he said words which for centuries have been part of evening prayer:

> *Lord, now let your servant depart in peace as*
> *you have promised,*
> *For with my own eyes I have seen the Saviour*
> *which you prepared in the sight of all people*

> *To be a light to give light to the Gentiles,*
> *and to be the glory of your people, Israel.*

An old man and an old woman were the first to acknowledge that this baby was the one they had spent their lives hoping for, the Saviour that all Jews hoped for. Simeon, after his own joyous recognition of the infant, promised Mary nothing easy; a sword would go through her own heart, he prophesied. And Mary must have turned cold inwardly.

But she was young enough to be able to accept difficult demands with courage, and to know that the way of the world is not always the way of the Lord.

> *The Lord is King, and hath put on glorious*
> *    apparel;*
> *The Lord hath put on his apparel,*
> *And girded himself with strength.*

But not the kind of glorious apparel or worldly power that might have been expected.

> *Like every newborn, he has come from very far.*
> *His eyes are blinded by the brilliance of the star.*
> *So glorious is he, he goes to this immoderate*
> *    length*
> *To show his love for us, discarding power and*
> *    strength.*
> *Girded for war, humility his mighty dress,*
> *He moves into the battle wholly weaponless.*

We don't know much about Jesus' early life. It's likely his father taught him carpentry, and this would have developed his muscles and helped to make him a strong man. His mother must have marvelled at him, wondered about the angel who came to her to announce his birth, and the the birth itself, with the shepherds coming to bring their humble gifts, and the kings their magnificent ones.

—*ML'E*

# On Knitting a Garment, and a Life

*JOURNAL, JANUARY 2, 1987*

I'm making some progress at last on my new project—the sweater I promised to knit for my friend Candace. She paid a lot for the yarn, and I must admit it is a joy to work with—dark charcoal grey with slate blue and black fibers, and flecks of red and blue and green. It is heavy—that is, it has heft; it feels substantial as it inches through my fingers onto the needles.

The pattern is a continental one translated, very badly, from Italian to English, which makes it ambiguous and confusing. Added to that, the yarn shop owner made some adjustments for this particular yarn, which is not the yarn the pattern calls for. The woman's scribbled writing is too indistinct to read easily. It's incomplete as well—she doesn't follow through consistently, leaving me with a lot of guesswork.

What this all means is that I must be my own designer. The photo of the sweater helps; what sounds impossible in the printed instructions becomes clearer when I can see the pictured shape and the patterned textures, knit without seams, all in one piece. Nevertheless, I've started it and ripped it out at least four times, using different sized needles and numbers of stitches to get the size and shape right.

I am feeling, in the roughness of the yarn as the garment grows in my hands, and from the repetitious click of the metal needles, what it is like, also, to knit a life. How experimental it is; how the instructions are not always intelligible and often make no sense until I knit them into reality, doing it over and over until it's right; how when I first start a pattern I can't discern the effect I'm working toward, but I follow the general idea anyway and see what happens and adapt as necessary, and finally something interesting and warm and beautiful takes shape under my fingers.

A slow process, stitch added to stitch, row to row, the work picked up and put down at odd moments the way one adds to one's own life by fits and starts. Single as I am, widowed after thirty-three years of marriage, I know that I'm knitting a new project, a major one, as big as this long, bulky jacket of Candy's, no incidental sock or collar. For all my wedded years I have knitted traditional Aran fisherman sweaters—complex, certainly, with convoluted cables and ribs and popcorns and honeycombs and trees and mosses and seed stitches, but recognizable within their genre. But this pattern is all new, the style unique. There will be no other sweater just like this, and though I have a pattern of sorts, my own trial and error and decision and will shape it into my own creation. I don't know yet what it will look like, finished. But the effort *feels* worthwhile.

I am both knitter and knitted one. I can see myself taking shape, all my yarns and fibers looped in rows that hold together and capture within them the tiny pockets of air that insulate and comfort the body—the air is part of the pattern, plained and purled into the pieces. Knitted stitch by stitch, hour by hour, it will take all of the years of my life to finish. Lord, I hope it looks good when it's done—a seamless garment.

## J A N U A R Y   4

Saw the following quoted in *Christianity Today,* from Walter Wangerin: "Faith is work. It is a struggle. You must struggle with all your heart. . . . And on the way, God will ambush you."

A poem by George MacDonald spoke to me gently along the same lines:

*O Son of man, to right my lot*
*Naught but thy presence can avail;*
*Yet on the road thy wheels are not,*
*Nor on the sea, thy sail.*

*My fancied ways, why should'st thou heed?*
*Thou com'st down thine own secret stair—*
*Com'st down to answer all my need,*
*Yea, every bygone prayer.*

As I visit my son John in Pensacola, the sun is shining so se-
ductively that I spread a sleeping bag on his narrow balcony and,
in spite of the wintry forty-five degrees, I put on my swimsuit
and luxuriate like a cat in a sheltered spot. I have felt so washed-
out looking, winter-white of skin. But more than a tan, my skin
simply welcomes the naked heat of the sun. For two contented
hours I have lain in it, knitted, read, dozed, meditated, particularly
on the MacDonald poem.

Again, as so often before, I felt the secret thoughts rising in
me, trusting them to be God-thoughts making themselves known.
Which started me reflecting on the Spirit, and how he teaches us
all things and guides us into truth, as Jesus promised. I read in
Paul's letter to the Corinthians about how God reveals things to
us—My spirit knows my thoughts, God's Spirit knows God's
thoughts. Because I am God's daughter, a bridge, a path, a secret
stair has been built from his heart to mine so that by the Spirit
God's thoughts can step into my mind. "This is what we speak,
not in words taught us by human wisdom, but in words taught
by the Spirit . . . The spiritual person makes judgments about
these things" because she has "the mind of Christ (NIV)." Even
these journal words are part of the process—this mysterious inner
inter-weaving of observation and reflection and verbalization.

As I lay there in the sun, thinking these thoughts as they came,
not trying to be "creative," the wind suddenly gusted and I saw
a scatter of gold leaves flying down from the maple saplings a
few yards away beyond the stream. (In Pensacola, fall comes in
January!) I have been wanting to take a photo to illustrate my

poem ". . . let him hear," about leaves falling from the trees at God's command because they hear him more attentively and obey him more instantly than we do. The image there in front of me was perfect. I brought my camera to the porch, focused, framed, and waited for the wind to blow again and release more leaves for my shutter. Talk about waiting for the Spirit (wind, breath) to stir. That was my literal task. My skin told me when the breeze was beginning, my ears could hear the tinkle of the wind chimes from the porch below. I took shot after shot, and only time and Kodak will tell my success or failure. But the lesson of waiting for the Spirit to move, watching, sensing the "now," obeying the breath, catching him at it, was learned whether or not a perfect image printed itself on the film.

I knew experientially my powerlessness to make the moment happen. A tree can't thrash its branches; it waits for the wind to move them. I can manufacture neither poems nor spiritual power, but my task is to be on the spot, watching, ready when the breeze picks up.

—LS

# A Call to Jury Duty

I n the late afternoon, when the long December night had already darkened the skies, we opened Christmas cards, taking turns, reading the messages, enjoying this once-a-year being in touch with far-flung friends. There, incongruously lying among the Christmas greetings, was an official-looking envelope addressed to me, with Clerk of Court, New York County, in the upper left-hand corner. A call to jury duty. Manhattan does not give its prospective jurors much notice. My call was for the first week in January. To the notice inside had been added the words *Must Serve*.

It wasn't the first time that my call had read *Must Serve*. A few months earlier I had written from Minnesota to the Clerk of Court, New York County, explaining that I was not trying to avoid jury duty, that I had previously served on a panel under a fine woman judge, and that I was ready and willing to serve again. But I pointed out, as I had already done several times before, that I do a good bit of lecturing which takes me far from New York, and I gave the Clerk of Court several dates when I would be available, sighing internally because bureaucracy never called me on the weeks that I offered.

This time they did.

So I relaxed and enjoyed Christmas in the country, at

Crosswicks, bitter cold outside, warmth of firelight and candle-light within, and laughter and conversation and the delectable smells of roasting and baking. One of the highlights came on Christmas Day itself, with the mercury falling far below zero, when my husband went out into the winter garden and picked brussels sprouts, commenting as he brought them in triumphantly, "Mr. Birdseye never froze them like this," and we had brussels sprouts out of our own garden with Christmas dinner.

And then, before Twelfth Night, I was back in New York again, taking the subway downtown to the criminal court to which I had been assigned. I took plenty of work with me, because I had been told that lawyers do not like writers. But just as had happened on my previous jury duty, I got chosen as a juror on the second day. The case was an ugly one, involving assault in the second degree, which means possession of a dangerous weapon, with intent to cause injury or death.

Two men were sitting in the courtroom as defendants. They looked at the twelve of us who had been told to stay in our seats in the jury box—looked at us with cold eyes, with arrogance, even with contempt. Later, as we jurors got to know each other, we admitted that we were afraid of them. And yet, according to our judicial system, we had been put in the position of having to decide whether or not, according to the law, these men were guilty as charged.

I was fortunate to serve again under a highly intelligent woman judge, who warned us that we must set aside our emotions. What we felt about the defendants should not enter into our deliberations. We should not form any preconceived opinions. "And remember," she told us, "these two men and their lawyers do not have to prove to you that they are innocent. They do not have to appear on the witness stand. The burden of proof is on the assistant district attorney. The American way is that these two men are innocent, unless it can be proved, beyond a reasonable doubt, that they are guilty. This is the American way." She also pointed out that this assumption of innocence unless guilt can be proven is not the way of the rest of the world, of countries behind the Iron Curtain or in much of South America, where the assumption is that you are guilty unless, somehow or other, by persuasion or bribe, you can prove your innocence.

When I was called for jury duty, I knew that I would be taking two long subway rides each day, and riding the subway in Manhattan is nothing one does for pleasure. So I picked up a small book from one of my piles of Books To Be Read Immediately. Why did I pick this book at this particular time? I don't know. But I have found that often I will happen on a book just at the time when I most need to hear what it has to say.

This book couldn't have been more apt. It was *Revelation and Truth*, by Nicholas Berdyaev. I didn't do much reading the first day because I was sent from court to court, but once I was on a jury and had long periods of time in the jury room, I opened the book, surrounded by my fellow jurors who were reading, chatting, doing needlework or crossword puzzles. There couldn't have been a better place than a criminal court in which to read Berdyaev's words telling me that one of the gravest problems in the Western world today is that we have taken a forensic view of God.

Forensic: *to do with crime*. I first came across the word in an English murder mystery. Forensic medicine is medicine having to do with crime. The coroner needs to find out if the victim has been shot, stabbed, or poisoned. Was the crime accidental, self-inflicted, murder? Criminal medicine.

And there I was, in a criminal court, being warned by a Russian theologian that God is not like a judge sentencing a criminal. Yet far too often we view God as an angry judge who assumes that we are guilty unless we can placate divine ire and establish our innocence. This concept seemed especially ironic after the judge's warning that this is not the American way of justice.

How did the Western world fall into such a gloomy and unscriptural misapprehension?

I suspect there may have been a lingering shadow of God as a cold and unforgiving judge—not a judge who believes in the American way, but one who assumes our guilt.

But no, Berdyaev states emphatically, no, that is not God, not the God of Scripture who over and over again shows love for us imperfect creatures, who does not demand that we be good or virtuous before we can be loved. When we stray from God, it is not God's pleasure to punish us. It is God's pleasure to welcome us back, and then throw a party in celebration of our homecoming.

God says through the prophet Hosea,

> *All my compassion is aroused,*
> *I will not carry out my fierce anger,*
> *I will not destroy Ephraim again,*
> *for I am God, not man:*
> *I am the Holy One in your midst,*
> *and have no wish to destroy.*

The nature of God does not fluctuate. The One who made us is still the Creator, the Rejoicer, the Celebrator, who looks at what has been made, and calls it good.

After the guard summoned us from the jury room to the court room, I sat in the jury box and looked at those two men who were there because they were destroyers rather than creators. They had used sharp knives, destructively; their intention had been to injure, or kill. I wasn't at all sure I wanted to be at the same celebration with them. They both had long hair, one head dark and greasy, the other brown and lank. They looked as though they had strayed out of the sixties, hippies who had grown chronologically, but not in any other way. It was difficult to abide by the judge's warning and not form any opinion of them until all the evidence was in.

That evening I was tired, mentally as well as physically. I bathed, then sat in my quiet corner to read Evening Prayer. For the Old Testament lesson I was reading the extraordinary story of Jacob's ladder of angels ascending and descending, linking earth and heaven, the Creation and the Creator, in glorious interdependence.

God stood above the ladder of angels, and said:

*I am the Lord God of Abraham, your father, and the God of Isaac: the land that you are lying on, to you will I give it, and to your seed. And your seed shall be as the dust of the earth. . . . And behold, I am with you, and will keep you in all the places where you go, and will bring you again to this land, for I will not leave you, until I have done that which I have said.*

*And Jacob woke out of his sleep, and he said, Surely the Lord is in this place, and I knew it not.*

*And he was afraid, and said, How dreadful is this place! This is none other than the house of God, and this is the gate of heaven.*

For Jacob the house of God was not a building, not an enclosure, but an open place with earth for the floor; heaven for the roof.

So Jacob took the desert stone he had used for a pillow and upon which he had dreamed the angelic dream, and set it up for a pillar, and poured oil upon the top of it. Oil—precious, sacramental.

How glorious stars must have been all those centuries ago when the planet was not circled by a corona of light from all our cities, by smog from our internal combustion engines. Jacob, lying on the ground, the stone under his head, would have seen the stars as we cannot see them today. Perhaps we have thrown up a smoke screen between ourselves and the angels.

But Jacob would not have been blinded to the glory of the stars as part of the interdependence of the desert, the human being, the smallest insects, all part of Creation.

If we look at the makeup of the word disaster, dis-aster, we see *dis,* which means separation, and *aster,* which means star. So dis-aster is separation from the stars. Such separation is disaster indeed. When we are separated from the stars, the sea, each other, we are in danger of being separated from God.

That January evening after the first tiring day as a juror, after I had read the story of Jacob and the angels, I turned to the New Testament, to read from the ninth chapter of Matthew's Gospel, where Jesus had called Matthew from collecting taxes. In Israel in those days, a tax collector worked for the hated Romans, rather than for an equivalent of the I.R.S. We don't have any analogy for the kind of tax collector Matthew was. But because they were employed by the enemy, all tax collectors were scum.

Nevertheless, incredibly, Jesus called Matthew to be one of his disciples, and that night he went for dinner to his house, where there were more tax collectors, and various other kinds of social outcasts, and the censorious Pharisees asked the disciples, "Why does your master eat with tax collectors?"

Jesus heard the question and said, "It is not the healthy who need a doctor, but the sick. Go and learn the meaning of the words, *What I want is mercy, not sacrifice.*" He was quoting from the prophet Hosea. And he went on, "And indeed I have not come to call the virtuous, but sinners."

I'm uneasy about self-conscious virtue. It implies that the virtuous person is in control, keeps all the laws, has all the answers, always knows what is right and what is wrong. It implies a conviction which enables the virtuous person to feel saved, while the rest of the world is convicted.

Probably it was because I was on jury duty that I noticed the paradoxical connections between the words conviction, convince, convicted, *con*vict (noun), and con*vict* (verb). If we assume that we are virtuous, particularly when we set our virtue against someone else's sin, we are proclaiming a forensic, crime-and-punishment theology, not a theology of love. The Pharisees who did not like to see Jesus eating with sinners wanted virtue—virtue which consisted in absolute obedience to the law.

The Pharisees were not bad people, remember. They were good. They were virtuous. They did everything the Moral Majority considers moral. They knew right from wrong, and they did what was right. They went regularly to the services in the temple. They tithed, and they didn't take some off the top for income tax or community services or increased cost-of-living expenses. They were, in fact, what many Christians are calling the rest of us to be: good, moral, virtuous, and sure of being saved.

So what was wrong? Dis-aster. Separation from the stars, from the tax collectors, the Samaritans, from the publican who beat his breast and knew himself to be a sinner. The Pharisees, not all of them, but some of them, looked down on anybody who was less moral, less virtuous than they were. They assumed that their virtue ought to be rewarded and the sin of others punished.

If we twelve jurors found those two men guilty as charged, they would be punished by the state. They would likely be put in prison: forensic punishment. Necessary in our judicial system, perhaps, but Berdyaev warned that we should not think of God's ways as being judicial. God is a God of love.

When I looked at those two cruel-faced men I had to remind myself that they were God's children, and that they were loved. If they had committed the crime of which they were accused, it would cause God grief, not anger.

I sat in the jury room with the radiators hissing and the January cold pressing against the windows, hearing the constant sound of taxis and busses and cars honking on the streets below.

I'm not at all sure that the state's forensic punishment is punishment at all. It may be deterrence, or an attempt to protect the innocent. I have no desire to go all wishy-washy and bleeding-heart about the rapist who is let off with an easy sentence so that he can then go out and rape and kill again, as statistics prove is almost inevitable. Our jails may be deplorable, our courts over-crowded and years behind schedule; our lawyers are not knights in shining armour; but we do what we can, in our blundering way, to curb crime and violence, and our top-heavy system remains one of the best on the planet.

But our own need for law and our system of prosecution and sentencing does not produce true punishment, because true punishment should result in penitence. Real punishment produces an acceptance of wrongdoing, a repugnance for what has been done, confession, and an honest desire to amend. Real punishment comes to me when I weep tears of grief because I have let someone down. The punishment is not inflicted by anyone else. My own recognition and remorse for what I have done is the worst punishment I could possibly have.

Perhaps the most poignant moment for me in all of Scripture comes after Peter has denied Jesus three times, and Jesus turns and looks at him. That loving look must have been far worse punishment for Peter than any number of floggings. And he went out and wept bitterly.

Jacob, too, learned to weep bitterly, but he was an old man before he came to an understanding of himself which included acceptance of repentance without fear.

This is something a criminal court is not equipped to cope with. The judge and the lawyers and the jurors are there to learn the facts as accurately as possible, and to interpret them according to the law. Forensically.

It is impossible to interpret the story of Jacob in this way. Jacob does outrageous things, and instead of being punished, he is rewarded. He bargains with God shamelessly:

*"If* God will be with me, and will keep me in this way that I go, and will give me bread to eat, and raiment to put on, so that I come again to my father's house in peace; *then* shall the Lord be my God."

Jacob also agrees to tithe, but only if God does for him all that he asks. He cheats, but he knows that he cheats; he never tries to fool himself into thinking that he is more honest than he is. He openly acknowledges his fear of Esau's revenge.

And yet, with all his shortcomings, he is a lovable character, and perhaps we recognize ourselves in him with all his complexity. He has an extraordinary sense of awe—an awe which does not demand fairness, an awe which is so profound a response to the Creator that it cannot be sustained for long periods of time.

But whenever El Shaddai came to Jacob, he was ready for the Presence. That was why he took his stone pillow and built an altar. Jacob knew delight in the Lord in a spontaneous manner which too many of us lose as we move out of childhood. And because we have forgotten delight, we are unable to accept the golden light of the angels.

Three centuries ago Thomas Traherne wrote:

*Should God give himself and all worlds to you, and you*

*refuse them, it would be to no purpose. Should He love you and magnify you, should He give His son to die for you, and command all angels and men to love you, should He exalt you in His throne and give you dominion over all His works and you neglect them, it would be to no purpose.*

*Should He make you in His image, and employ all His Wisdom and power to fill eternity with treasures, and you despise them, it would be in vain. In all these things you have to do; and therefore all your actions are great and magnificent, being of infinite importance in all eyes; while all creatures stand in expectation of what will be the result of your liberty. . . . It is by your love that you enjoy all His delights, and are delightful to Him.*

As I live with Jacob's story I see that there is far more to him than the smart cheat, the shallow manipulator. There are many times when he so enjoyed the delights of God, that he himself became delightful.

How often are we delightful to God? How marvellous that we are called delightful!

We are not meant to cringe before God. We are to enjoy all the delights which the Lord has given us, sunsets and sunrises, and a baby's first laugh, and friendship and love, and the brilliance of the stars. Enjoying the Creator's delights implies connectedness.

And so there is hope that we, too, may so enjoy all the delights that God has given us, that we may truly be delightful.

—ML'E

# Snowfall

On Riverside Drive
only the sleds move; New Yorkers
are learning to toboggan a slope
on a kayak, a pizza box.

The front page of the *New York Times*
is a blizzard of photos; Times Square
a white desert. Cars, like coffins under
their palls of snow, line 94th Street.
Along Broadway a handful of pedestrians
lean into the wind, mere smudges
in the camera lens, ignoring
the green yellow red, green yellow red
blinking at non-existent taxi-cabs;

Skyscrapers haunt the city—
each tall ghost shrouded in flurries.
When the air clears—thin
and startling as crystal—
the frozen buildings still gaze at us,
windows like blank eyes. In a chilled
apartment building a woman sits,
warmed by the white cat in her lap.

—*LS*

# QUILTMAKER

*"I make them warm to keep my family from freezing; I
make them beautiful to keep my heart from breaking."*
—*prairie woman, 1870*

To keep a husband and five children warm,
she quilts them covers thick as drifts against
the door. Through every fleshy square white
    threads
needle their almost invisible tracks; her hours
count each small suture that holds together
the raw-cut, uncolored edges of her life.

She pieces each one beautiful, and summer
    bright
to thaw her frozen soul. Under her fingers
the scraps grow to green birds and purple
improbable leaves; deeper than calico, her
    mid-winter
mind bursts into flowers. She watches them
    unfold
between the double stars, the wedding rings.

—*LS*

# MOVING TOWARDS LENT

It is still winter. Today has seen a quick flurry of snow followed
by blue skies and sunshine. We are moving towards Lent and
then the glory of Easter, that most marvelous holy day that radi-
antly bursts through the limitations of fact.

—*ML'E*

## REVEALING STRUCTURE

Strangely I have found in my own life that it is only through a wintry spirituality that I am able to affirm summer and sunshine. A friend wrote me recently, "Winter reveals structure." Only as the structure is firmly there are we able to dress it with the lovely trappings of spring, budding leaves, rosy blossoms. Winter is the quiet, fallow time when the earth prepares for the rebirth of spring. Unless the seed is put into the ground to die, it cannot be born.

—*ML'E*

## A PROMISE OF SPRING

It's cold and clear, but there's a promise of spring as I look out the window and down the street where the trees in Riverside Park are faintly blurred against the sky as they are losing their winter starkness and are preparing to bud. I'm ready for new green and warmer breezes. Bion tells me that at Crosswicks the green shoots of daffodils have pushed up through the snow.

—*ML'E*

# FAITH

Spring is a promise
in the closed fist
of a long winter. All
we have got is a raw
slant of light at a low
angle, a rising river
of wind, and an icy rain
that drowns out green
in a tide of mud. It is
the daily postponement
that disillusions. (Once
again the performance
has been cancelled by
the management.) We live
on legends of old
springs. Each evening
brings only remote
possibilities of
renewal: "Maybe
tomorrow." But the
evening and the morning
are the umpteenth day
and the God of sunlit
Eden still looks
on the weather
and calls it good.

*—LS*

## NEW BIRTH:
## HEART SPRING

often after easter
last summer's deep
seeds rebel
at their long frozen sleep
split, swell
in the dark under
ground, twist, dance
to a new beat
push through a lace of old
pale roots

invited by an unseen heat
they spearhead up, almost
as though, suddenly,
their tender shoots
find the loam light
as air
not dense, not sodden cold

I saw a crocus once
in first flight
stretching so fast
from a late snow
(a boundary just passed
a singular horizon close below)
the white cap melt-
ing on its purple head

such swift greening of leaf wings
and stalk was clear celebration
of all sweet springs
combined
of sungold
smell of freshness, wind
first-time felt

light lifting, all new things
all things
good and right and all the old
left behind

—*LS*

## CALLING, CALLING

One foggy night I was walking the dogs down the lane and heard the geese, very close overhead, calling, calling, their marvellous strange cry, as they flew by. I think that is what our own best prayer must sound like when we send it up to heaven.

And indeed prayers continue and will continue. Mostly my prayers are almost wordless, just a holding out to God of your names, and then I can call on the Spirit, like the geese.

—*ML'E*

Lord Jesus, in this fateful hour
I place all Heaven with its power
And the sun with its brightness
And the snow with its whiteness
And the fire with all the strength it hath
And the lightning with its rapid wrath
And the winds with their swiftness along their
   path
And the sea with its deepness
And the rocks with their steepness
And the child in the manger
Sharing our danger
And the man sandal-shod
Revealing our God
And the hill with its cross
To cry grief, pain, and loss
And the dark empty tomb
Like a Heavenly womb
Giving birth to true life
While death howls in strife
And the bread and the wine
Making human divine
And the stars with their singing
And cherubim winging
And Creation's wild glory
Contained in His story
And the hope of new birth
On this worn stricken earth
And His coming, joy-streaming
Creation redeeming
And the earth with its starkness

---

*This poem is based on and incorporates "The Rune of St. Patrick."

All these we place
By God's Almighty Help and grace
Between ourselves and the powers of darkness.

—*ML'E*

## Prayers for Peace

We send you all our prayers for peace in our hearts and in the world, for an end to terrorism and famine, and for the birth of hope and loving connections among all people.

—*ML'E*

# Acknowledgments

Many of the pieces in this book are previously unpublished and are used by kind permission of Madeleine L'Engle and Luci Shaw.

Grateful acknowledgment is made to the following publishers for permission to use these works:

BY MADELEINE L'ENGLE:

"Joyful in the newness of the heart" from *The Anglican Digest* (Pentecost 1983). Reprinted by permission.

"Redeeming All Brokenness" and "Revealing Structure," from Madeleine L'Engle's introduction to *Awaiting the Child: An Advent Journal* by Isabel Anders. Copyright 1987 by Isabel Anders Throop. Reprinted by permission of Cowley Publications and Isabel Anders.

"'Anesthetics,'" from A CIRCLE OF QUIET. Copyright © 1972 by Madeleine L'Engle Franklin. Reprinted by permission of Farrar, Straus & Giroux, Inc.

"This Extraordinary Birth," "Forever's start," "After annunciation," "A Galaxy, a Baby," "That Newness," "The Promise of His Birth," "In Human Flesh," "The birth of wonder," "A Time of Hope," "The Eve of Epiphany," "The Light of the Stars," "Atomic Furnaces," "Soaring," from THE IRRATIONAL SEASON. Copyright © 1977 by Crosswicks, Ltd. Reprinted by permission of Farrar, Straus & Giroux, Inc.

"Miracle on 10th Street," from *Life* (December 1991). Reprinted by permission of the author.

"This tiny baby" (from "The Baby in the Bath"), "Tree at Christmas," "For Dana" (originally titled "For Dana: 4th November"), from LINES SCRIBBLED ON AN ENVELOPE. Copyright © 1969 by Madeleine L'Engle Franklin. Used by permission of Farrar, Straus & Giroux, Inc.

"A Full House: An Austin Family Story" (originally titled "A Full House"), from *McCall's* (December 1980). Reprinted by permission of the author.

The poem contained in "The Glorious Mystery" beginning, "This is no time for a child to be born" was previously published as "The Risk of Birth" in *The Risk of Birth,* copyright 1974 by Harold Shaw Publishers. Used by permission.

"Eighty-second Street," "Chamonix," "Saying Yes," "A Deepening Vision," from THE SUMMER OF THE GREAT-GRANDMOTHER. Copyright © 1974 by Crosswicks, Ltd. Used by permission of Farrar, Straus & Giroux, Inc.

BY LUCI SHAW:

"Yes to Shame and Glory," *Christianity Today* (December 12, 1986). Used by permission. The poem within this article, beginning, ". . . We have seen the